Credits & Copyright

All-in-One Applications, a dba of SJG Professional Communications, Inc., feels honored to have participated in the creation of such revolutionary materials. We want to thank Bryan Contreras, not only for giving us this opportunity to fulfill a dream, but also for providing inspiration, support, and wisdom.

Coursework designed and authored by

Jessica Givens, Jamil Driscoll, & Errolynn Zetar

ISBN: 0-9845964-3-7

Copyright © 2012
Houston, TX

SJG Professional Communications, Inc.
1129 W Pierce
Houston, TX 77019

TURN THE TABLES ON THE TEST-MAKERS

Introduction

HOMEWORK

Date	Assignment

WELCOME

Welcome to the All-in-One Applications Elite SAT/ACT Foundations Course

What are we going to do here ?

We're going to lay a practical foundation for your <u>foray</u> into standardized test preparation.

We're going to start with the _____ because it's really the more basic exam.

What does the SAT test ?

<u>Ostensibly</u>, it tests Writing, Reading, and Math.

Reading = _____ and _____

Writing = _____ and _____

Math = _____, _____, _____, and _____.

In actuality, it tests your ability to _____.

Some people are <u>innately</u> good test-takers; some people aren't. Whichever category describes your testing <u>propensities</u>, you can and will get better. And, that's why we're here.

How are we going to change the course of your test taking destiny ?

We're going to turn the tables on the test makers.

What do test makers expect testers to do ?

Attack questions _____

Try to do _____

With the SAT, this is usually the ***wrong*** approach. Why? Because on the SAT, there is a

_____. The scoring goes like this:

Right answer: +1

Wrong answer: - ¼

Blank answer: 0

_____

" In other words, if you're totally <u>befuddled</u> by a question, you probably don't want to put down an answer. You'll increase your score by answering questions *strategically*. "

MAJOR RULES

1

- All the questions on this test are worth the same amount (1 possible point).

- The questions come in three varieties: Easy, Medium, and Hard.

- You don't have to be a hero. Get the Easy and Medium questions right. If you have to skip the hard ones, do it with pride. No one will ever know.

2

- If you know an answer is incorrect, cross it out. Why leave it there to taunt you?

- Once you've eliminated 2 answers, you can reasonably take a stab at the answer.

- Keeping your pencil moving is the only way to stay engaged. No passive test taking!

3

- We are going to come up with an individual pacing chart for you. Follow it.

- Know how many questions you should do in a section.

- Success on this test is all about remaining calm and working the system to your advantage.

BASIC FACTS

Scoring

- Each section is scored out of 800.

- The scores are added together to reach a maximum cumulative score of 2400.

- Colleges will almost always take the highest possible total score.

There are 10 Sections

	# of 25-min. sections	# of 20-min. sections	Total
Math	2	1	3
Reading	2	1	3
Writing	2	1	3
			9

" So, where does that 10th section come in? Well, it's what ETS calls the *experimental section*, and it can come in any of the SAT flavors – Math, Reading, or Writing. "

- **Is the experimental section scored?** _____

- **Why is it there?** 2 reasons:
    > To test out new questions
    > To torture students

- **Can you skip it?** Sure, if you know which section it is, which you won't. So, _____ .

TOTAL NUMBER OF QUESTIONS: 54 Math   67 Reading   49 Writing   1 Essay

More About Scoring....

Here's a clearer picture of this scoring business. If you want a certain score, here's the number of raw points you're going to need:

	800	750	700	650	600	550	500	450	400
Math	54	52	47	44	38	32	25	19	12
Reading	67	63	59	53	46	38	29	21	14
Writing	49	44	40	36	31	27	22	17	11

Don't bite off more than you can chew in the beginning:
You have the luxury of a little time here. Pick an initial goal score and strive for that. Don't shoot for the stars from the outset. Preparing for the SAT is all about measuring progress.

You are unlike anyone else, right? So, why should you test like anyone else?

You need a unique testing strategy that matches your aptitudes.

On that note, let us welcome your most trusty sidekick on this test, your Pacing Planners.

These planners are merely samples, but we are going to have you create your own. And, for each homework we assign, we want you to time yourself and follow your Pacing Planner. You will tweak the numbers as you progress!

PACING PLANNERS

		Math			
	25 minutes	25 minutes		20 minutes	65 minutes
To get:	20 question problem solving	8 question problem solving	10 question grid-in	18 question problem solving	Total
400	6	3	4	5	18
450	9	3	4	6	22
500	10	4	5	7	26
550	14	5	5	10	34
600	16	6	7	13	42
650	18	7	8	16	49
700	20	8	10	18	54
750	20	8	10	18	54
800	20	8	10	18	54

- Math is a little more consistent than Reading. You always know how many questions you'll have in each individual section.

- In Reading and Writing, they feel no qualms about switching things up at will. Sometimes, your 25-minute sections will have 24 questions; sometimes, they'll have 26.

		Reading								
To get a score of	25 minutes			25 minutes			20 minutes		Total questions to answer	Total points needed
	5 qn SC	Short RC	Long RC	8 qn SC	Short RC	Long RC	6 qn SC	Whammy RC		
400	2	4	5	2	4	5	2	6	20	14
450	2	4	6	3	4	5	2	6	32	21
500	2	4	8	4	4	7	3	8	40	29
550	3	4	11	5	4	9	4	10	50	38
600	4	4	12	7	4	10	5	10	56	46
650	4	all	all	7	all	all	all	all	65	53
700	all	all	all	all	all	all	all	all	ALL 67	59
750	all	all	all	all	all	all	all	all	ALL 67	63
800	all	all	all	all	all	all	all	all	ALL 67	67

Where do you stand???

Every time you take a test, you want your personal pacing planner (yes, your PPP) in mind. We're putting a few in here, so you can make plans for homework, your practice test, and your first real-deal exam. If you take extra tests on your own, modify this pacing planner. Don't abandon it. <u>This</u> is where progress begins!

What's your current goal score for Math? _____

So, how does that line up with your pacing planner??? Give it a shot:

20 question problem solving	8 question problem solving	10 question grid-in	18 question problem solving	Total

And your goal score for Critical Reading? _____

Now, plan that:

25 minutes			25 minutes			20 minutes		Total questions to answer
5 qn SC	Short RC	Long RC	8 qn SC	Short RC	Long RC	6 qn SC	Whammy RC	

....

No, we don't dwell on the writing score. It's just not that important, and we're going to shoot for the stars there in any case!!

YOUR PPP's

"**On every homework assignment, you need to time yourself.** It's just the way it is. You need to keep track of multiple numbers. You also need to circle the questions you didn't understand and ask them in the classroom."

That's why we're here!

Homework #1

Math

Total number of questions	Number to attempt	Number correct	Number incorrect	Total points

# of problem solving: _____ # of grid-ins: _____

Reading

Total number of questions	Number to attempt	Number correct	Number incorrect	Total points

Math

Total number of questions	Number to attempt	Number correct	Number incorrect	Total points

# of problem solving: _____   # of grid-ins: _____

Reading

Total number of questions	Number to attempt	Number correct	Number incorrect	Total points

Math

Total number of questions	Number to attempt	Number correct	Number incorrect	Total points

# of problem solving: _____   # of grid-ins: _____

Reading

Total number of questions	Number to attempt	Number correct	Number incorrect	Total points

Math

Total number of questions	Number to attempt	Number correct	Number incorrect	Total points

# of problem solving: _____ # of grid-ins: _____

Reading

Total number of questions	Number to attempt	Number correct	Number incorrect	Total points

Math

Total number of questions	Number to attempt	Number correct	Number incorrect	Total points

# of problem solving: _____ # of grid-ins: _____

Reading

Total number of questions	Number to attempt	Number correct	Number incorrect	Total points

Practice test plans for Math and Reading:

Test 1

Math

20 question problem solving	8 question problem solving	10 question grid-in	18 question problem solving	Total

Reading

25 minutes			25 minutes			20 minutes		Total questions to answer
5 qn SC	Short RC	Long RC	8 qn SC	Short RC	Long RC	6 qn SC	Whammy RC	

Test 2

Math

20 question problem solving	8 question problem solving	10 question grid-in	18 question problem solving	Total

Reading

25 minutes			25 minutes			20 minutes		Total questions to answer
5 qn SC	Short RC	Long RC	8 qn SC	Short RC	Long RC	6 qn SC	Whammy RC	

THE REAL DEAL

What are you planning?

Math

20 question problem solving	8 question problem solving	10 question grid-in	18 question problem solving	Total

Reading

25 minutes			25 minutes			20 minutes		Total questions to answer
5 qn SC	Short RC	Long RC	8 qn SC	Short RC	Long RC	6 qn SC	Whammy RC	

TURN THE TABLES ON THE TEST-MAKERS

SAT
ACT

Mathematics

MATHEMATICS

BREAKDOWN...

There are 3 Math Sections

Section I (18 Questions: 25 Minutes)

Multiple Choice	Questions 1 - 8
Grid In	Questions 9 - 18

Section II (20 Questions: 25 Minutes)

Multiple Choice	Questions 1 - 20

Section III (16 Questions: 20 Minutes)

Multiple Choice	Questions 1 - 16

>>>>> The sections are not always in this order <<<<<

(1) Leave your ego at home

(2) Numbers! Numbers! Numbers!

(3) Pick Numbers that make sense

(4) Your Calculator = Best Friend

(5) Master the "First Half"

(6) Write Stuff Down

(7) Break down word problems

(8) Pick... Don't Ever Guess

(9) "Tail End" Questions

(10) Handling the "Last Ones"

1

- Test writers prey on students who think they are above simple arithmetic questions and using a calculator to find the answer to 13 times 6 or 1/3 of 126.

2

- If you were given a million dollars to solve one of the following questions, which would you pick?

A. $x + y = ?$

B. $3 + 4 = ?$

- Numbers never change. A 4 will always and forever be a positive 4. An x can be anything - integer, negative, fraction, another variable, etc.

3

- The entire SAT math section can be completed without a calculator (something we are not going to do, remember technique #1). Still, we want to always use numbers that are easy and logical.

- Based on the question type, we can start with easy integers and see how that helps.

- **Zeros and Ones are special**, as we will see, so we want to be cautious when those come along.

>>> EXAMPLE

A car travels 200 miles in x hours…

x = _____

4

- We always want to use a calculator not only to solve problems but to check our answer too.
- Knowing how to effectively use parentheses, powers, fractions, graphing, and other cool functions, we can make our lives so much easier.
- Students think that it will take too much time to solve five equations, but the calculator lets you do it in a manner of seconds.

$$\frac{\left(-\frac{1}{3}\right)^{(9-5)}}{(6+2)}$$

$$\frac{3}{64} \qquad -\frac{1}{32} \qquad \frac{9}{119} \qquad \frac{1}{648} \qquad -\frac{3}{648}$$

Calculator Quick Tip:

Convert decimals to fractions using the button:

MATH: >FRAC

## 5

- Since the line of questioning always gets harder, you should master the first part of the section.
- Remember, the first question counts just as much as the last one. These are the easiest points that we **never** want to give away through carelessness, ego, or speed.

If $3(x + y) + 5 = 23$, then $x + y =$

(A) 4

(B) 5

(C) 6

(D) 7

(E) 8

COUNTS JUST AS MUCH AS:

At the cafeteria, there was one hamburger for every 3 freshmen, one apple for every 6 freshmen, and one milk for every 8 freshmen. If the total number of hamburgers, apples, and milks was x then, in terms of x, how many freshmen were at the cafeteria?

(A) $\frac{9}{8} x$

(B) $\frac{4}{3} x$

(C) $4 x$

(D) $\frac{8}{5} x$

(E) $24 x$

6

- Even if you are overwhelmed, you can pull some information to begin to put together a math problem.
- If it says there are 43 girls in a classroom, we write that down and start there.
- If we don't write our information down, you will spin your wheels, burn valuable time, and become frustrated.

7

- Whenever we see a period or a comma, we pause. Try to transcribe somewhere the information given in that sentence or phrase.
- They give you a ton of space around the problem and we intend to use it all. Even if it's as simple as "let x be a positive , odd integer," we write down "x = 5"

> The interior dimensions of a rectangular box are 10 feet long, 4 feet wide, and 3 feet high. This box is filled to the top with bubble wrap. All of the bubble wrap in this box is taken out and placed into a smaller, second box. If the interior dimensions of the second box are 6 feet long, 6 feet wide, and 2 feet high, what could be the dimensions of a third box that will be filled to the top with the amount of bubble wrap that was not able to fit into the second box?

Piece 1: _____

Piece 2: _____

Piece 3: _____

8

- The test makers want you to guess, and we don't want to do anything they intend for us to do, right.
- If we can logically eliminate two of the answers, we "pick" between the last three.
- **You are always better off skipping than guessing.** Remember, we want to use our resources to get closer to an answer instead of guessing at an answer because it looks good.

9

- Remember, they're jerks, so it's not surprising that they will try to trick you at the end of the question.
- Always check the last phrase of the question, making sure that it matches what they're asking.
- **Beware of phrases like, "what is 2x" or "what is half of x"**

If $x = 2$ is a solution of the equation $x^2 + 5x + c = 0$, what is the value of $2c$?

(A) - 14

(B) - 10

(C) 1

(D) 14

(E) - 28

- The last three questions are **always** the hardest. They involve the most calculations and seven times out of ten, the answer choices are cleverly chosen to make you pick the wrong one.
- If you feel confident that you got it right, think again because the numbers are not in your favor that you correctly answered the question.
- Many students do not even bother looking at the last two or three in the 20 or 16 MC sections and spend that time devoted to the first half.

DID YOU KNOW   (?)

It is still possible to get a perfect score on the math section even if you skip a couple of problems.

MATHCABULARY

- You thought that you only need to know vocab for the Verbal sections, but you need to know it for math.

- On average, each section will contain 2 or 3 questions that incorporate direct understanding of vocab.

"Math questions require you to know some vocab, or you will be lost and guessing - and that's never what we want."

TYPE	DEFINITION	EXAMPLE
Integer		
Positive		
Negative		
Even		
Odd		
Prime		
Factor		
Multiple		
Remainder		
Distinct		
Consecutive		

Operation	Mathcab the test-makers use:
+	
—	
X	
÷	

OTHER MATHCAB TO KNOW

>> PEMDAS: _____

>> Absolute value: _____

>> **M**ean: _____

>> **M**edian: _____

>> **M**ode: _____

Number Sets   {-9, 5, -6, 3, 3, 11, 13}

  >> Union:
  >> Intersection:

REMEMBER:

hundre**ds** | tens | units | ten**ths** | hundred**ths** | thousand**ths**

135.246

Turning the Tables: Plugging In

> Mary is three times as old as George and five years younger than Alexis. If George is g years old, how old is Alexis, in terms of g?
>
> (A) $g + 5$
>
> (B) $g + 3$
>
> (C) $2g$
>
> (D) $3g - 5$
>
> (E) $3g + 5$

Don't Forget: **Numbers, numbers, numbers!**

Pick a number for g: _____   How old is Alexis? _____

>>> That's a lot easier than freaking out about an algebra equation.

" Any time you see the phrase "IN TERMS OF" you should start plugging in numbers. "

PLUGGING IN STEPS

1. Read the entire question first

2. Label clearly everything you plug in

3. Always circle your goal answer

4. Go through all the answer choices

If $a \neq 0$, and $a = 3b = 5c$, what is the value of $a + b$ in terms of c?

(A) 5c

(B) 3c

(C) $\frac{20}{3}$ c

(D) 15c

(E) $\frac{3}{5}$ c

a = _____   b = _____   c = _____

Goal answer: ☐

Remember tip #3 - pick numbers that make sense. Since we are multiplying by 5s and 3s, we want to use multiples of those numbers

If x flapjacks cost 10 cents, what is the cost, in cents, of y flapjacks at the same rate?

(A) xy/10

(B) 10y

(C) 10x/y

(D) 10x

(E) 10y/x

If a, b, and c are consecutive odd integers, and c > b > a, then in terms of a, c equals?

(A) a + 1

(B) a + 2

(C) a - 2

(D) a + 4

(E) a - 4

Picking numbers out of thin air

>>> Sometimes a problem won't have variables, but still beg for plugging in

>>> Usually, those problems will have fractions or percents in them

For Tom's birthday, his mom bakes him a cake. That night, Tom eats 1/4 of the cake. The next morning, his mom eats 1/2 of what remains. What fraction of the cake remains uneaten?

(A) 3/4

(B) 1/8

(C) 1/4

(D) 5/8

(E) 3/8

Mastering Word Problems

>>> Sometimes, you will have to write an equation

Have no fear, as long as you break up the word problem and label properly, you'll be fine.

In a primate exhibit, there are 14 more orangutans than chimps. If there are 70 primates in the exhibit, how many orangutans are there?

(A) 42

(B) 44

(C) 48

(D) 52

(E) 56

>>> In many cases, you'll have to write more than one equation, but they are not hard!

>>> Let's review some algebra mathcab!

3 more than 4: _____

5 less than 11: _____

6 less than 2 times 5: _____

REMEMBER
THE THING AFTER "THAN" ALWAYS COMES FIRST!

Dealing with TWICE, HALF, and HAS.

John has twice as many shoes as Mary: _____

RULE: "HAS IS THE EQUAL SIGN"

Maria has one-third as many peanuts as Neil: _____

Michael is 15 years older than Patrick. In ten years, Michael will be twice as old as Patrick. How old is Michael today?

(A) 15

(B) 20

(C) 25

(D) 30

(E) 40

Alberta has twice as many handbags as Makiko. If Alberta gave Makiko 6 handbags, she would have four fewer handbags than Makiko would then have. How many handbags did Alberta have before she gave Makiko 6 bags?

(A) 6

(B) 14

(C) 16

(D) 18

(E) 20

Were those examples really hard **?**

>>> If so, there's another way...

> For many word problems, you can actually turn the tables on the test makers by manipulating the answer choices. "

>>> Let's try it with the last two examples.

What does the answer to question 1 represent? _____

How can we get Patrick's age from Michael's age? _____

How many years are added in the question? _____

How can we get Michael and Patrick's ages after that time? _____

At the end, how should their ages compare? _____

>>> Starting with answer choice (C), let's get to work:

	Now	Plus 10 Years
Michael		
Patrick		

	Now	Plus 10 Years
Michael		
Patrick		

	Now	Plus 10 Years
Michael		
Patrick		

If a and b are integers and ab is an odd integer, which of the following must be an even integer?

(A) $a + b + 3$

(B) $3ab$

(C) ab

(D) $a + b$

(E) $\dfrac{a + b}{3}$

If peanuts can be bought for p cents per pound, how many pounds of peanuts can you buy for $6?

(A) $\dfrac{6}{p}$

(B) $600p$

(C) $\dfrac{60}{p}$

(D) $\dfrac{p}{600}$

(E) $\dfrac{600}{p}$

If 8 more than $2x$ is two less than y, what is the value of y in terms of x?

(A) $x + 5$

(B) $2(x + 8)$

(C) $2(x + 10)$

(D) $2(x + 5)$

(E) $\dfrac{1}{2}(x + 10)$

George, John, and Paul buy a boat. Paul pays twice as much as John and half as much as George. If John pays x dollars, in terms of x, how much does the boat cost?

(A) $3x$

(B) $\dfrac{7x}{2}$

(C) $2x$

(D) $5x$

(E) $7x$

If 3 more than x is 3 times y, what is the value of y in terms of x?

(A) $x + 3$

(B) $3x + 3$

(C) $\dfrac{x + 3}{3}$

(D) $\dfrac{x + 6}{3}$

(E) $\dfrac{1}{3}x + 3$

A group of teenagers are sharing the $90 cost of a hotel room. If an additional person were to join them, the cost would go down by $1 per person. How many people are currently in the group?

(A) 6

(B) 9

(C) 10

(D) 12

(E) 15

GEOMETRY

TRIANGLES

>> Area = _____

>> Perimeter = all the sides _____

>> The sum of the angles is _____

>> The longest side is opposite the _____ angle

>> The shortest side is opposite the _____ angle

>> Equal sides are opposite _____ angles

TYPES OF TRIANGLES

>> Isosceles:

_____ angles are equal

The sides opposite the _____ angles are _____

>>>

>> Equilateral:

_____ angles are equal

_____ sides are equal

>> Every angle equals _____

>> Can be divided into two _____ triangles

For right triangles, don't forget the Pythagorean Theorem!

• _____ + _____ = _____

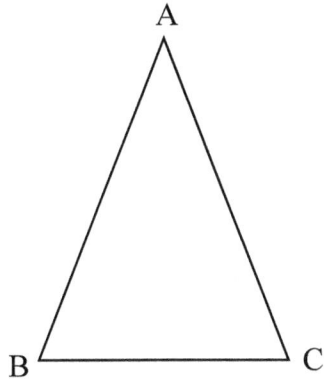

Note: Figure not drawn to scale

Triangle ABC is isosceles. If <ABC = 35°, what is one possible value of <CAB?

(A) 120°

(B) 90°

(C) 75°

(D) 50°

(E) 35°

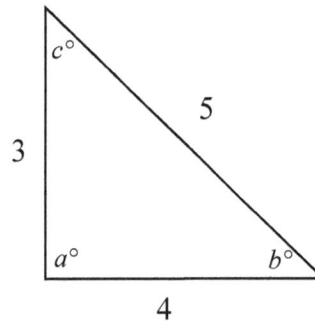

Which of the following must be true of a, b, and c in the figure above?

(A) $a < b < c$

(B) $b < a < c$

(C) $b < c < a$

(D) $c < b < a$

(E) $c < a < b$

Who remembers the 30°-60°-90° triangle ratio? It could come in handy on the above problem!

Just for practice, write it here: _____

In $\triangle DEF$, $DE = EF = DF$, and $DE = 12$. What is the area of $\triangle DEF$?

(A) 144

(B) $72\sqrt{3}$

(C) 72

(D) $36\sqrt{3}$

(E) 36

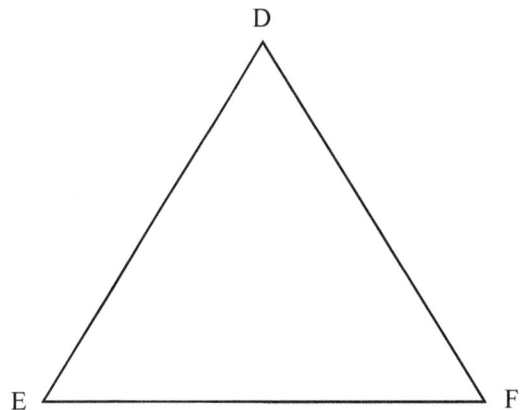

QUADRILATERALS

In any 4 sided figure, the sum of the angles is _____

Squares:

Area = _____

Perimeter = _____

_____ sides are equal

Every angle equals _____

Squares can be divided into two _____ triangles

Rectangles:

Area = _____

Perimeter = _____

Opposite sides are _____

All angles equal _____

Rectangles can be divided into two _____ triangles

Parallelograms:

Area = _____

Opposite sides are _____ and _____

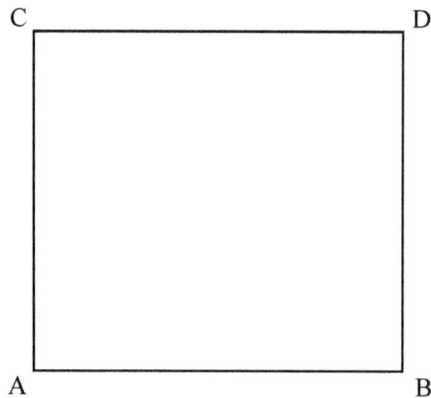

The area of square ABCD is 100. What is its perimeter?

(A) 100

(B) 90

(C) 60

(D) 40

(E) 10

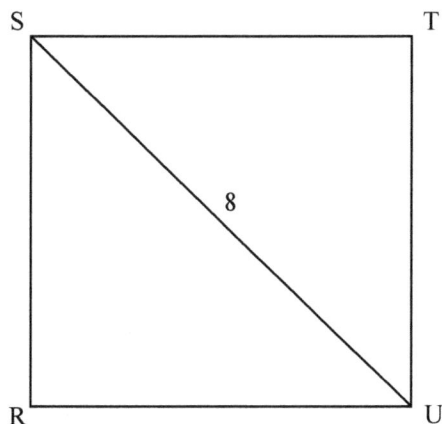

In square RSTU above, if diagonal SU = 8, what is the area of the square?

(A) $64\sqrt{2}$

(B) 64

(C) $32\sqrt{2}$

(D) 32

(E) $16\sqrt{2}$

Now, here we are with a 45°-45°-90° triangle. How do we know? Well, we are given a **square**.

What's the ratio for these triangles? _____

COMBINING CONCEPTS

(Of <u>course</u>, you can plug in on Geometry!!)

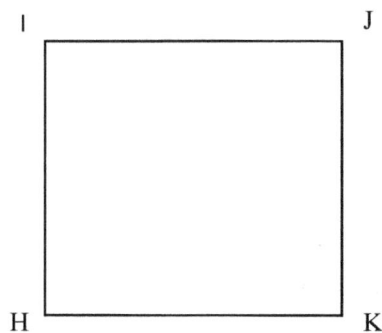

The area of square ABCD is x. In terms of x, what is the length of diagonal IK?

(A) $\sqrt{2}x$

(B) $x\sqrt{2}$

(C) $2\sqrt{x}$

(D) $2x$

(E) $4\sqrt{x}$

CIRCLES

There are _____ degrees in a circle

Area = _____

Area is how much _____ there is in the circle

Circumference = _____

Circumference is really the _____ of the circle

Diameter:

The _____ line in a circle

Passes through the _____ of the circle

Touches both _____ of the circle

Radius:

Halfway across the circle

Equal to _____ the diameter

More intricate circle vocab:

Tangent lines:

Touches a circle in exactly _____

Always forms a _____ angle to something

Notorious on harder SAT questions

Chord:

Any _____ from one part of the circle to another

The _____ is the longest chord

Arc:

A portion of the _____

Can be used in FULL FRAC proportions

Sector:

A portion of the _____

Can be used in FULL FRAC proportions

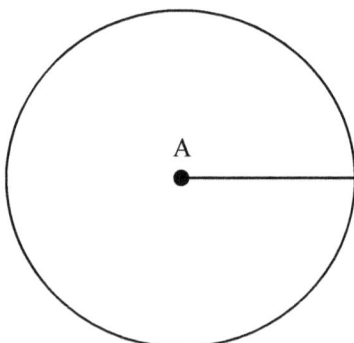

Let's do a little practice:

- If Circle A has a radius of 12, what's the diameter? _____
- If Circle A has an area of 36π, what's the radius? _____
- If Circle A has a diameter of 14, what is the area? _____
- If Circle A has an area of 169π, what is the circumference? _____
- If Circle A has a circumference of 18π, what is the area? _____

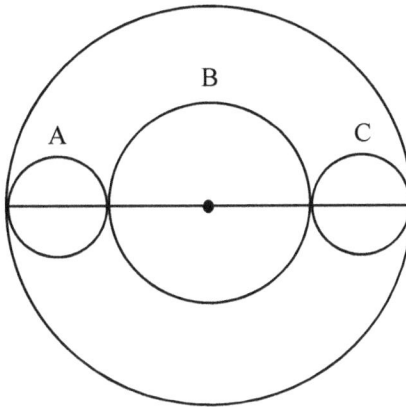

In the figure above, the circles are tangent as shown, and the center of circle B is also the center of the outside circle. If the radius of circle B is 8, the radius of circle A is 4, and the radius of circle C is 4, what is the radius of the outside circle?

(A) 8

(B) 10

(C) 12

(D) 14

(E) 16

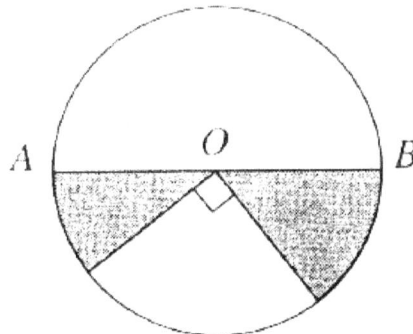

In the figure above, the circle with center O has a radius of 8. If AB is the diameter of O, what is the area of the shaded region?

(A) 2π

(B) 4π

(C) 8π

(D) 16π

(E) 32π

Hello, Triangle. May I introduce you to my good buddy, Circle?

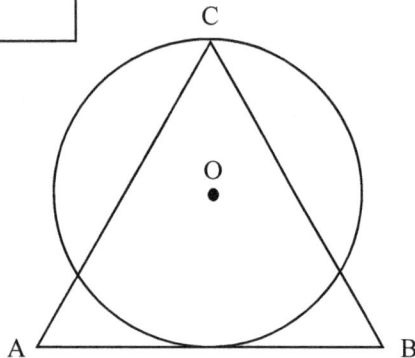

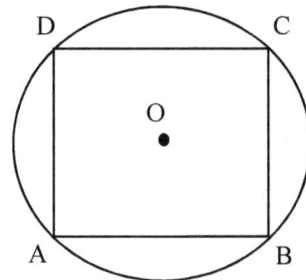

In the figure above, $AB = BC = AC$, and the area of the circle with center O is 144π. What is the area of triangle ABC?

(A) $\dfrac{8\sqrt{3}}{3}$

(B) $8\sqrt{3}$

(C) $\dfrac{16\sqrt{3}}{3}$

(D) $16\sqrt{3}$

(E) $192\sqrt{3}$

In the figure above, given that the area of square ABCD is 8. What is the circumference of the circle with center O?

(A) 2π

(B) $2\pi\sqrt{2}$

(C) 4π

(D) $4\pi\sqrt{2}$

(E) 8π

PARALLEL LINES

You may have hated them in school, but on the SAT, they're easy-peasy.

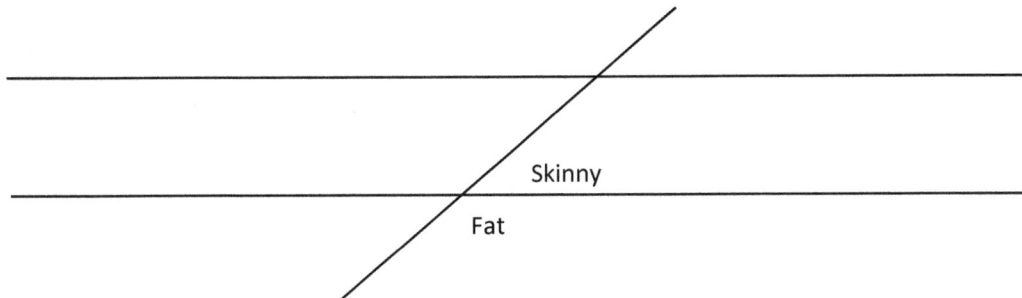

Skinny

Fat

In SAT land, nobody bothers with fancy names, like corresponding and alternate interior. Nope, we've boiled it down to this: Fat and Skinny. All the fat angles are equal. All the skinny angles are equal. Fat + Skinny = 180°. Period.

If you want high-falutin' geometry, go somewhere else. To turn the tables, leave that ego at the door!

Since parallel lines are pretty easy, test-makers like to mess kids up by disguising the parallel-ness!

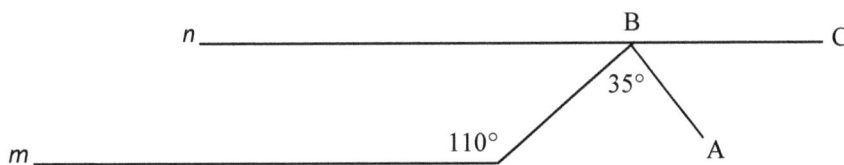

n ———————— B ————— C
            35°
m ———————— 110°   A

In the figure above, given that line *m* is parallel to line *n*, what is the value of ∠ABC?

(A) 35°

(B) 55°

(C) 65°

(D) 75°

(E) 85°

Oh, you silly little SAT! You think I can't find the area of a shaded region. Think again!!

The SAT test-makers have mastered the art of taking little shapes you know very well and putting them on top of each other to make something that looks completely foreign. We've spotted their tricks, though, so the madness ends today!!!!

To find the area of a scary shaded region, you just need to do this:

Area of the big shape — Area of the little shape = Area of the shaded region

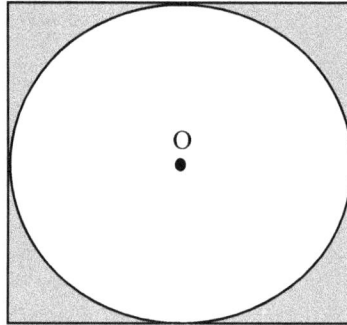

Given that the circle with center O has a radius of 5, find the area of the shaded region.

(A) 25π

(B) $50 - 12\pi$

(C) 50π

(D) $100 - 25\pi$

(E) 100π

The Test-Makers are at it again! They're using circles on steroids to destroy students' confidence.

Still, as usual, they are predictable. On complicated circles, think **FULL FRAC!**

FULL: In practically every case, you're going to have the information to find the circumference or area for the **full** circle.

FRAC: You'll also be given an angle measure or a percent that you can use to make a **fraction**.

FULL X FRAC = Your answer!

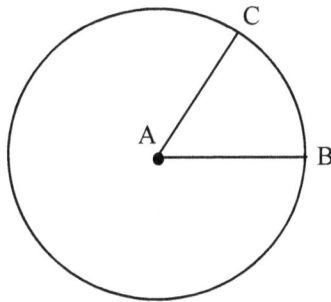

The circle with center A has a radius of 12. If ∠ BAC has a measure of 60°, what is the area of sector ACB?

(A) 6π

(B) 12π

(C) 24π

(D) 36π

(E) 48π

Okay, we're talking about AREA here. Let's get some facts together.

Full Area = _____

Frac = $\dfrac{Angle}{360°}$

So, (FULL) (FRAC) = _____

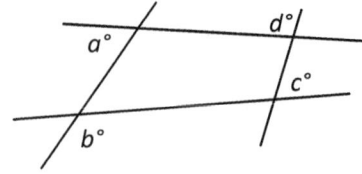

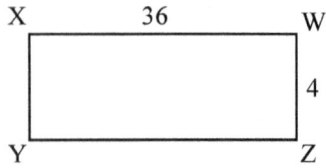

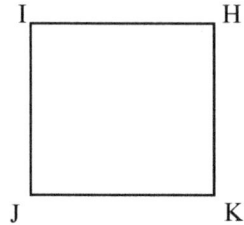

If quadrilateral HIJK is a square and its area is equal to that of rectangle WXYZ, what is the length of side JK?

(A) 4

(B) 8

(C) 12

(D) 16

(E) 20

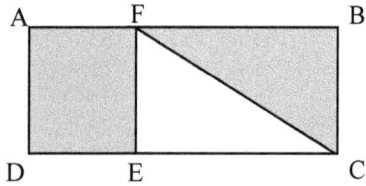

In the figure above, AD = BC = 4. If AB = 20, and EC = $\frac{3}{5}$ DC, what is the area of the shaded region?

(A) 12

(B) 24

(C) 38

(D) 49

(E) 56

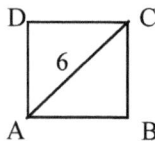

What is the area of square ABCD?

(A) 6√2

(B) 18

(C) 18√2

(D) 36

(E) 36√2

What is the sum of a, b, c, and d in the figure above?

(A) 180°

(B) 240°

(C) 360°

(D) 400°

(E) 540°

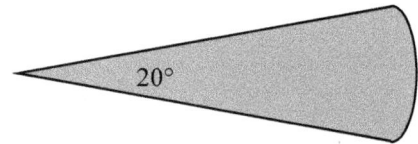

The pie wedge above has a radius of 18. What is the area of the wedge?

(A) 324π

(B) 162π

(C) 81π

(D) 18π

(E) 9π

ARITHMETIC

Turning the Tables on Middle School Math

Averages are easy, right? Well, the SAT tries to make them hard. You have to turn the tables to stay a step ahead of the game.

There are 3 parts to every average problem:

1. _____

2. _____

3. _____

You always need <u>all three</u>!!!

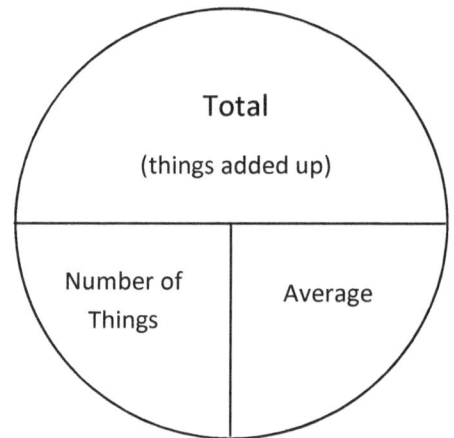

Total
(things added up)

Number of Things

Average

In her algebra class, Jane got a 98, 87, 74, and 92 on her first four tests, respectively. Her parents tell her that she needs a 90 or above in the class if she wants to maintain a semblance of a social life. What does she need to get on her fifth test to meet that goal?

(A) 91

(B) 93

(C) 95

(D) 97

(E) 99

Draw one of those Average Circles each time you see the word average in a problem. You could have as many as four. Who cares?! Just keep drawing!

A group of 12 students compared their scores on a history exam. They found that the average of the entire group was a 91. The five highest scoring students had an average of 98. What was the average of the other 7 students?

(A) 90

(B) 87

(C) 86

(D) 78

(E) 75

THINK!!!

How many times does the word average come up in the question?

That's how many circles you need to draw!!

The average of x and y is 18. What is the average of x, y, and 24?

(A) 16

(B) 18

(C) 19

(D) 20

(E) 24

PROPORTIONS

Remember Proportions??? Yep, that Four Square is here to stay.

On the SAT and ACT, you can use it with everything from basic comparison problems to rates to ratios.

The most important thing to keep in mind with proportions, ratios, etc. is that you need to be consistent. If on one side you put miles on top and hours on the bottom, you have to do the same thing on the other side. Don't get creative. And don't forget to cross-multiply.

A recipe for 12 chocolate chip cookies calls for 6.5 cups of sugar. Maria wants to make 288 cookies. How many cups of sugar does she need?

Cookies	Cookies
Cups of sugar	Cups of sugar

Mary-Kate buys 3 bags of carrots each day. If each bag of carrots weighs one pound, and one pound is 16 ounces. How many ounces of carrots has she purchased at the end of 365 days?

(A) 48

(B) 195

(C) 1040

(D) 3120

(E) 17520

A snow cone machine produces 4 liters of shaved ice in 15 seconds. How many liters can it produce in 5 minutes?

(A) 20

(B) 80

(C) 100

(D) 150

(E) 300

THINK!!!

Tricky test makers switching up the units!

" Ratios throw a small fly into the ointment because you sometimes need to **add them up!** If you see that they mention a **total**, you need to add your ratio up and use *that* in your **Four Square.** "

A summer camp accepts boys and girls in a ratio of 3:5. If there are 120 total kids at the camp, how many are boys?

(A) 12

(B) 24

(C) 45

(D) 60

(E) 75

A jar holds cashews, almonds, and brazil nuts in a ratio of 3:5:7. If there are x cashews in the mix, then, in terms of x, how many total nuts are in the jar?

(A) $3x$

(B) $5x$

(C) $7x$

(D) $12x$

(E) $15x$

VARIATION

>>>> It comes in two forms, **direct** and **inverse**.

In **direct variation**, we use the basic proportion setup: $\dfrac{x_1}{y_1} = \dfrac{x_2}{y_2}$

If x varies directly with y, and $x = 3$ when $y = 11$, what is the value of y when $x = 24$?

(A) 22

(B) 33

(C) 55

(D) 88

(E) 121

In **inverse variation**, we spice it up a little with: $x_1 y_1 = x_2 y_2$

If r varies inversely with s, and $r = 8$ when $s = 14$, what is the value of r when $s = 28$?

(A) 2

(B) 4

(C) 12

(D) 14

(E) 112

>>> Complicating an uncomplicated topic:

> So, those simple equations for inverse and direct variation get majorly corrupted by the test makers. When you find yourself a potential victim of their shenanigans, you need to go back to the basic equations. Most importantly: **Don't be afraid to plug in!**

In a given situation, y varies directly with the square of x and inversely with the cube of z. What is the result, in terms of y, when x is doubled and z is halved?

(A) $32\,y$

(B) $\frac{1}{16}\,y$

(C) $\frac{3}{16}\,y$

(D) $\frac{1}{4}\,y$

(E) $\frac{2}{3}\,y$

PERCENTS

- Playing the "is over of" game with the Four Square

Let's make percents as easy as possible. Here's the deal: $\dfrac{\%}{100} = \dfrac{is}{of}$

In a box of 244 peanuts, 25% are shelled. How many peanuts are shelled?

(A) 25

(B) 38

(C) 61

(D) 122

(E) 183

Just put an *x* wherever you are missing a quantity!

What percent of 96 is 120?

(A) 125%

(B) 66%

(C) 75%

(D) 120%

(E) 200%

In a bag of Halloween goodies, 20% of the candy is M&M's, 15% of the candy is Snicker's Minis, 35% of the candy is Twizzlers, and the other 18 pieces are Reese's Pieces. How many pieces in total are in the bag?

(A) 36

(B) 44

(C) 54

(D) 60

(E) 72

" $\dfrac{\text{is}}{\text{of}}$ works with Geometry, too! "

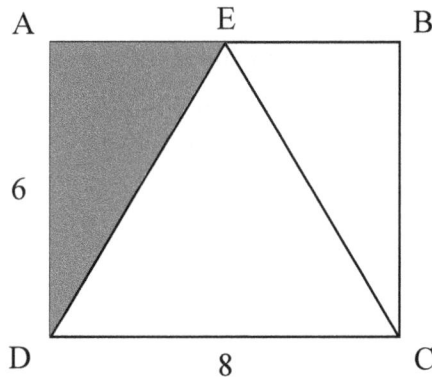

In the figure above, if E is the midpoint of segment AB, then the shaded region accounts for what percent of the total area?

(A) 10%

(B) 15%

(C) 20%

(D) 25%

(E) 75%

Patterns: It's all about repetition. We're going to set up a chart and do some counting and figure out where the pattern repeats.

Nadine is creating a playlist. She puts songs on in the following order of genres: Country, Blues, Rap, Jazz, Alternative, and Techno. What would the genre of the 79th song be?

(A) Country

(B) Blues

(C) Rap

(D) Jazz

(E) Techno

$$2.303003000300003000003\ldots$$

If the number above continues to follow the same pattern shown into infinity, how many zeroes will precede the 296th three?

(A) 294

(B) 295

(C) 296

(D) 297

(E) 298

"Freaky Functions! They're "Plugging In" in disguise!"

The SAT (not so much the ACT) has a habit of inserting bizarre shapes into the math section and tripping students up because they feel so caught off-guard. On these tests, even when you feel totally confused, the worst mistake is to stop moving your pencil. To turn the tables on those test-making jokers, you have to persevere and <u>keep writing</u>!

$$\Diamond x = x^2 - 2x^3 + 8$$

What is the value of $\Diamond 3$?

(A) 45

(B) 37

(C) 8

(D) -37

(E) -45

_____

Which of the following is equal to 13?

(A) $\Diamond 8 + \Diamond 5$

(B) $\Diamond 8 - \Diamond 5$

(C) $\Diamond 8 + \Diamond 4$

(D) $\Diamond 4 + \Diamond 5$

(E) $\Diamond 4 - \Diamond 5$

The average of a, b, c, and d is 18. What is the average of $a - 6$, $b + 10$, $c - 20$, and $d + 4$?

(A) 12

(B) 15

(C) 18

(D) 24

(E) 28

Aaron buys six bundles of asparagus in one day. If each bundle has 3 dozen asparagus spears in it, how many spears does Aaron buy? (Note: 1 dozen = 12 spears)

(A) 18

(B) 36

(C) 72

(D) 180

(E) 216

The ratio of red marbles to blue marbles in a magician's bag is 4:3. If there are 16 red marbles in the bag, how many total marbles are in the bag?

(A) 12

(B) 15

(C) 18

(D) 24

(E) 28

At the airport, a group of students going on a study-abroad program is split into two groups to go through security. In the first group, the security stops 20 percent of the students. In the second group, security stopped 35 students. If a total of 85 students were stopped, how many students were in the first group?

(A) 100

(B) 150

(C) 200

(D) 250

(E) 300

The number of textbooks a school bookstore sells varies directly with the number of students on campus. If, in 2009, a school with 3,844 students sold 1,922 textbooks, then how many students were at a school that sold 4,805 books?

(A) 5,766

(B) 9,610

(C) 10,571

(D) 11,532

(E) 17,298

If $\langle\!\langle x \rangle\!\rangle = 3x^2 + 4x$, then what is the value of:

$$\langle\!\langle 4 \rangle\!\rangle + \langle\!\langle 3 \rangle\!\rangle$$

(A) 7

(B) 18

(C) 80

(D) 95

(E) 103

FUNCTIONS & GRAPHS

>>> Breaking down f(x) into parts:

Two parts:

1. The stuff inside the parenthesis

2. The entire function

This can be either f, g, h, p or any other letter of the alphabet

USING YOUR PENCIL

1. Determine what number and where you will place your pencil:

Inside parenthesis is *x axis*

$$f(3) = k$$

right side of equal sign is *y axis*

$$f(x) = 5$$

2. Place your pencil on the appropriate axis at that point.
3. Slide your pencil until you hit the graph.
4. This answer will be the value of the part you are trying to find

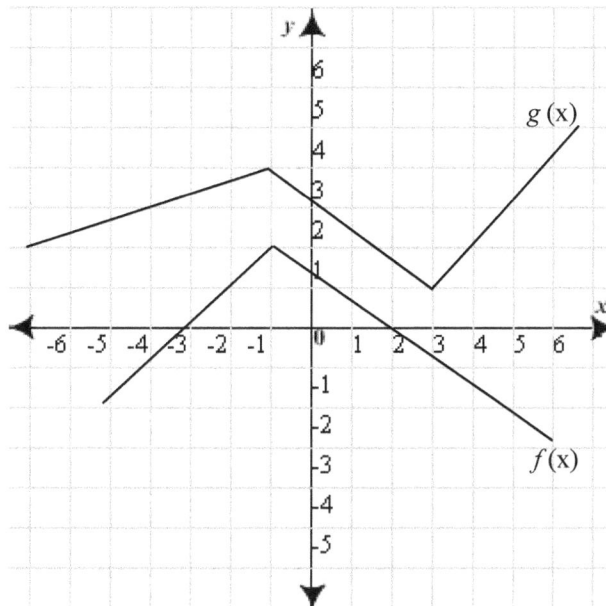

Figure out what number we're trying to find

$f(x) = 0$ _____

$g(x) = 4$ _____

$g(0) =$ _____

$f(4) =$ _____

>>> COMBINING OUR CONCEPTS <<<

Those above are pretty easy, right. Now, let's see how they can ask a question that makes you think a little harder.

Referring to the graph above, if $f(h) = 2$, what is one possible value of x that would make function $g(x) = h + 2$?

(A) -1

(B) 0

(C) 2

(D) 2.5

(E) 3

SLOPES, LINEAR, AND QUADRATIC FUNCTIONS

Equation for the slope of a line: _____

Parallel versus perpendicular lines: _____

If a line contains three points with coordinates (5,-3), (8,3), and (10, z), what is the value of z?

(A) 13

(B) 11

(C) 7

(D) 1

(E) -7

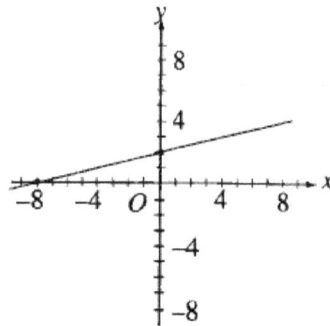

The graph above represents $f(x)$, which of the following could represent a line parallel to $f(x)$?

(A) $g(x) = -x + 4$

(B) $g(x) = 4x - 2$

(C) $g(x) = \frac{1}{4}x + 4$

(D) $g(x) = -4x + 4$

(E) $g(x) = -\frac{1}{4}x + 2$

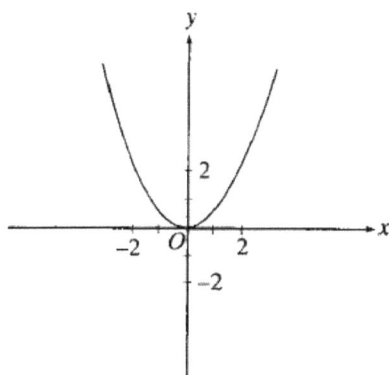

The graph of $y = f(x)$ is shown above. Which of the following is the graph of $y = f(x - 1) + 2$?

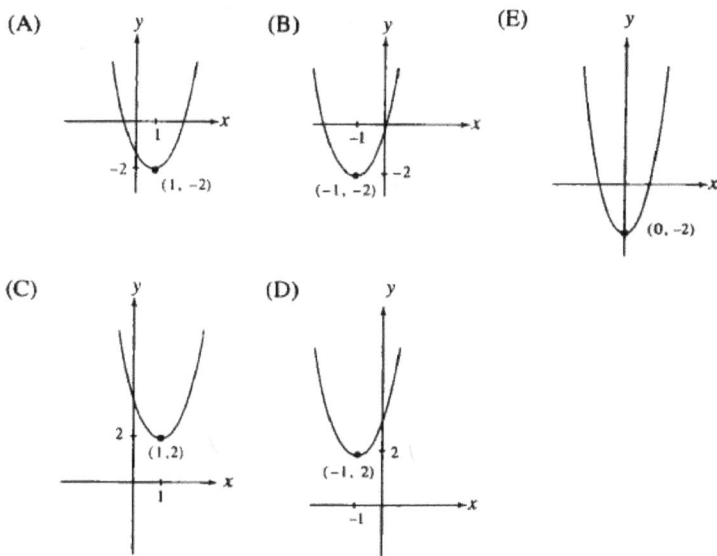

(A)

$(1, -2)$

(B)

$(-1, -2)$

(E)

$(0, -2)$

(C)

$(1, 2)$

(D)

$(-1, 2)$

Absolute value reminder: In most cases, you'll have two answers, so you'll want to check both because they will only have one correct answer.

If $|2x + 3| = 13$, which of the following values equals 0?

(A) $x - 8$

(B) $x - 5$

(C) $x - 13$

(D) $x + 5$

(E) $x + 13$

Critical Reading

CRITICAL READING

BREAKDOWN...

There are 3 Critical Reading Sections

Section I (25 Minutes)

Sentence Completions	Questions 1-5
Short Passages	Questions 6-9
Long Passages	Questions 10-24

Section II (25 Minutes)

Sentence Completions	Questions 1-8
Short Passages	Questions 9-12
Long Passages	Questions 13-24

Section III (20 Minutes)

Sentence Completions	Questions 1-6
This Section has NO Short Passages	
Long Passages	Questions 7-19

" Note: The test makers like to play switcheroo with the 25-minute CR sections, but the 20-minute section is a constant. "

In the land of SAT Verbal, there are 5 Table Turning Techniques that can give you the power to ace this test.

1

2

3

4

5

"Whether you're working on a Sentence Completion or plowing your way through a Double Whammy Passage, let those 5 simple rules guide your behavior."

Know them, love them, use them.

1 ELIMINATE "LIKE" FROM YOUR VOCABULARY

- The SAT writers are looking for certain answers.
- They do not particularly care about what you think about the passage or what you think at all.
- Chances are, the right answer will be one you don't like.
- You must learn how to spot incorrect answer choices, even if they look right to you.

2 BE COMFORTABLE WITH DISCOMFORT

- Get ready. You're going to have to pick some answers that make you queasy.
- The correct SAT answer is the *best* answer, the cream of the crap, so to speak.
- It's okay if you feel iffy about bubbling it in. Just do it.

3 PREDICT YOUR ANSWER FIRST

- SAT makers always include answer choices that look right but are not.
- You can avoid these "traps" by knowing what you're hoping to find in an answer.
- Using the passage as a guide, you should predict the correct answer then eliminate those that don't match up.

4   LEARN TO ELIMINATE EFFECTIVELY

- Here's a sad truth: just because you don't understand an answer doesn't mean it's wrong.
- You have to eliminate for a reason.
- That said, you need to eliminate like a fiend.
- Remember, there are four wrong answers and only *one* right answer. Get rid of some garbage before you commit!

5   DON'T FORGET YOUR PACING

- Remember our pacing chat!
- Don't do every question unless you're on the cusp of 700 land.

SENTENCE COMPLETIONS

- Sentence completions are not overly complicated. They are just fill-in-the blank questions you've answered all your life.

- The sentence completions come at the _____ of each Critical Reading Section.

- Arranged in order from easy to hard, the sentence completions contain either _____ or _____ blanks and _____ possible answer choices.

• •

In order to gain the maximum amount of points, you must learn these core strategies:

① _____

② _____

③ _____

④ _____

1   DON'T GET CREATIVE

- Creativity may be rewarded in English class, but it is punished on the SAT.
- The writers of the test think *as literally as possible*.
- They want you to choose the answer that works best, not the one that could work.
- Do not add extra details to rationalize an answer choice.

2   USE SENTENCE CLUES TO PREDICT ANSWERS

- Before looking at the answer choices, you're going to **predict** your answer.
- You may be thinking, "Easier said than done! They all look right!"
- Well, guess what? They're not all right. That's because each sentence has its own set of **clues** and **pivot points** that make one answer better than the others.

Turn the Table Technique: Move that Pencil

>>> Underline SC clues.

What's a clue? It's the part of the sentence that talks about the blank.

> Because of its close tie to American history, baseball is more than a sport in the United States; in fact, we see it as part of our national _____.

What's your clue here?

What word would you plug in the blank?

Which of these answer choices might work?

(A) Epiphany
(B) Curiosity
(C) Introspection
(D) Heritage
(E) Endeavor

>>> Circle Pivot Points.

What's a Pivot Point?

" A word or punctuation mark that affects the direction of a sentence.

They can either push the sentence in the _____ direction or switch things up by

going in the _____ direction. "

Examples of Common Pivot Points

Same direction	Opposite direction
:	Although
;	However
Consequently	But
Furthermore	Yet
Moreover	Nonetheless
And	Despite

3 — ELIMINATE WHAT WON'T WORK

- Strong test takers go into the questions looking for ways to get rid of answer choices.
- Don't go in trying to find the right answer first, eliminate what doesn't work.

4 — CHOOSE THE BEST ANSWER, THEN CHECK IT

- Pick the last man standing.
- Before you bubble in your choice, read it back into the sentence to see if the choice makes sense.

Okay... let's walk through one of the **medium difficulty** questions using the tips we've just discussed.

STEP:

1 >>> Read the sentence, noticing clue words, direction words, and/or punctuation

2 >>> Predict your answer

3 >>> Eliminate answer choices

4 >>> Pick the best one

28. David's request to borrow coffee was only a -------, a way to meet the new neighbors without being openly inquisitive.

    (A) misgiving   (B) requisition   (C) compunction
    (D) delusion   (E) pretext

1

Short on analysis but long on -------, the book is little more than a series of diverting stories.

(A) cliché   (B) prophecy   (C) pedantry
   (D) anecdote   (E) critique

>>

2

The republic's government became so ------- that during one three-week period five different presidents held office.

(A) irreproachable   (B) archaic   (C) tyrannical
   (D) clandestine   (E) precarious

>>

3

While not openly contemptuous, the comedian's comments about the city included such ------- insinuations that the audience was offended.

(A) idiosyncratic   (B) idealistic   (C) concise
   (D) banal   (E) demeaning

Each section of the sentence completions contains one or two **really challenging** questions. But don't fret; you can up your chances of answering them correctly.

● ●

Sentence Completions are difficult for 3 reasons

1

- This is the most common category of difficult sentence completions.
- The best way to handle these is preparation a head of time.

2

- Your first line of defense is to look for clue words and direction words that will help you with your predictions.

- Yet, some sentences are worded in ways that leave you with little clues to grasp. The structure can make these sentences seem unpredictable.

- You have a limited amount of time to answer a question, so you obviously want all sentence completions to be as short as possible.

- But, alas, some sentence completions can look like paragraphs. Don't panic, you can do this. Take the same steps you've learned for the easy ones. Break down the sentence into digestible chunks that will allow for a better grasp of its meaning.

" Try to have some type of **prediction** before looking at the answer choices. Remember, they aren't your friends and are not there to make your life easy.

Look for clues, relationships, charges, or paraphrasing.
<u>Anything that gives you an edge</u> "

Okay... let's walk through one of the **maximum difficulty** questions thinking about the reasons and steps we've discussed.

STEP:

1 >>> **Read the sentence, noticing clue words, direction words, and/or punctuation**

2 >>> **Predict your answer**

3 >>> **Eliminate answer choices**

4 >>> **Pick the best one**

Remember: Break down the sentence into digestible chunks

Although the clattering noise from the machinery did not -------, the workers eventually became ------- to it, hardly noticing it.

(A) reverberate . . accustomed
(B) persist . . drawn
(C) fade . . exposed
(D) cease . . hostile
(E) abate . . inured

1

Maxine Hong Kingston's *The Woman Warrior* -------
stories of women who are triumphant and stories of
those who are victimized, placing contrasting portraits
side by side.

(A) withholds   (B) supersedes   (C) complements
   (D) juxtaposes   (E) interrupts

>>

2

It was inevitable that the ethics committee would
------- the moral character of the candidate because
he was such a ------- individual.

(A) exonerate . . prurient
(B) notice . . recondite
(C) exalt . . malignant
(D) assail . . contrite
(E) impugn . . nefarious

>>

3

The sound produced by the youth orchestra was so
------- that even its least experienced members were
abashed.

(A) cacophonous   (B) syncopated   (C) harmonic
   (D) collaborative   (E) mellifluous

WHAT IF I DON'T KNOW THE WORDS ?

- There may be a couple of sentence completions per section that will contain very difficult vocabulary.

- Skip the question if you have no idea what most, if not all, of the words mean. **Time is of the essence on this test.**

- If your vocabulary skills are weak, your best bet is to answer <u>fewer sentence completions</u> so you can spend more time on the reading passages.

VOCABULARY

"Learning vocabulary is one of the most important aspects of test preparation.

It doesn't matter how many strategies you've perfected, if you don't know the words used, you cannot answer the questions correctly. Luckily, this is one of the easier skills to learn; you just need to devote some time to learn new words."

>>> HOW TO MASTER VOCABULARY <<<

There are several strategies you can employ that will help you learn new vocabulary.

First, though, let's look at the types of words the SAT writers use.

This is the most obvious category. The SAT makers choose words that you will run into in college. Think of these words as upper-level synonyms of words you already know.

> **EXAMPLES:** *loquacious* and *garrulous* are both synonyms for *talkative*.

>> STRATEGY

>> **Flashcards** - The best way to learn new words is to make flashcards. Put the unknown word on one side and the definition, plus one or two synonyms on the other.

>> **Quizlet.com** - This website offers thousands of online flashcard sets in all kinds of subjects. Just search "SAT Vocabulary" and select a few sets that you think are the best. Save and practice these sets as often as possible. Quizlet also creates tests for you to train your brain and make the entire process more fun.

>> **Novel SAT books** - If you go to the test prep section at Barnes & Noble or just search Amazon for "SAT novel" you'll find a ton of interesting books that will incorporate vocab into the story. Many students prefer this approach to flashcards because it is not as monotonous and helps to practice your reading comprehension at the same time

One trap that the SAT writers love to use is to use familiar words that have multiple meanings. Usually, these words are very familiar to you, yet you may only know one meaning.

EXAMPLES: Do you know both meanings of the following words:

Word	Meaning 1	Meaning 2
gravity		
confidence		
currency		
compromise		

>>> STRATEGY

These words are usually located in hard sentence completions. If there is a word that you immediately think is too easy to be in the answer choices, be careful, it might have another meaning.

Not very common, but worth mentioning. There are cases of words that are used in such specific situations that students lose sight of their true meanings.

EXAMPLES: Do you know the meaning of the following words:

Word	Meaning
discriminate	
fastidious	
exacerbate	
censure	

Remember, you have to understand the meaning of words and not just ways you are used to using them.

There is no expectation that you will know every word on the SAT. Some words will just be unfamiliar.

"A way to combat this is to learn word roots. Roots will help you with at least part of the definition, usually enough to help you eliminate the word if it doesn't work."

Prefix	Meaning	Examples & Definitions
a, ab, abs	away from	absent - not present abscond - to run away
ad, a, ac, af, ag, an, ar, at, as		
anti		
bi, bis		
circum, cir		
com, con, co		
de		
dis, dif, di		
epi		

Prefix	Meaning	Examples & Definitions
equ, equi		
ex, e, ef		
in, il, ir, im		
in, il, ig		
inter		
mal, male		
mis		
mono		
non		
ob		
omni		
poly		
pre		
pro		
re		
super		
trans		
un		

Roots	Meaning	Examples & Definitions
act, ag	to do, to act	Agent - a representative Activity - action
apert		
bas		
cap, capt, cip, cept, ceive		
ced, cede, cess		
curr, curs		
dic, dict		
duc, duct		
graph		
mit, mis		
par		
pon, pos, posit, pose		
scrib, cript		
sequ		
tact		
ten, tent		
ven, vent		
vert, vers		

Word	Prefix	Root	Meaning
concurrence	con: with	curr: run	Happening at the same time
exaggerate			
malediction			
precursor			

5 RELATED WORDS FROM DIFFERENT PARTS OF SPEECH

Have you ever seen a word that you didn't recognize but knew it looked like another word you knew?

For example, you may not recognize **erroneous** but doesn't it look like **error**? That's because *erroneous* is an adjective meaning *containing error*.

While this strategy doesn't work all the time (*equivocal* has nothing to do *with being equal*) it may help you when you feel like you've seen a word before.

These are usually found in the harder questions.

Okay... let's <u>delve</u> into some practice questions that will <u>engage</u> your vocabulary <u>faculties</u>.

STEP:

1 >>> **Read the sentence, noticing clue words, direction words, and/or punctuation**

2 >>> **Predict your answer**

3 >>> **Eliminate answer choices**

4 >>> **Pick the best one**

Citing evidence that babies shielded from harmful microbes during infancy may be ------- developing allergies as adults, the scientist claimed that excessive hygiene is -------.

(A) prone to . . deleterious
(B) exempt from . . immaterial
(C) resistant to . . obsolete
(D) protected from . . perilous
(E) predisposed to . . therapeutic

1

Peregrine falcons are among the avian world's great ------, sometimes migrating as much as 18,000 miles each year.

(A) mercenaries   (B) itinerants
   (C) charlatans   (D) recidivists
     (E) provincials

>>>

2

Feeling ------- by a voting process that ultimately led to their votes being invalidated, these citizens ------- their discontent by way of a lawsuit.

(A) heartened . . voiced
(B) emboldened . . denied
(C) compromised . . garnered
(D) disenfranchised . . registered
(E) intrigued . . revoked

>>>

3

Although many people in contemporary times choose to speak explicitly, the tradition of ------- is still very much alive.

(A) garrulousness   (B) exaggeration
   (C) excoriation   (D) oration
     (E) euphemism

READING PASSAGES

What you need to know

- You are about to embark on something that is totally different from what you've learned in school.

- We want to let you in on a little secret: **Standardized test creators are not your friends.** They are not in the business to make their tests easy to complete.

You have to put aside how you answer Critical Reading questions in English class

for the following reasons:

1 THEY DON'T CARE ABOUT YOUR OPINION

Your English teacher may love your interpretations of the classics in class but you will be doing yourself a disservice if you try that on the SAT. You are asked to read a passage and answer questions based on information gleaned from the passage, not to look for answer choices you like or think should be correct.

2 CREATIVITY IS NOT GOOD

We repeat: **Creativity is not good!** The SAT is written to be very literal. There is no room for inventing extra information that is not written in the passage. Even questions that ask you to infer, your inference should still come from what you read.

Remember we told you the writers aren't your friends. Every set of answer choices scream "choose me!!" They are the ones we usually hear students say "I just like that one." Or "It makes sense." Don't fall for that.

Turn the Table Techniques

1. **Don't read the passage in its entirety**. As we've said before, this is a timed test. You won't have enough time to read the entire passage and then answer the questions that follow.

2. **Read the italicized portion and the 1st 3rd of the passage**. Many times the italics at the beginning of a passage give you the main ideas of the passage. If you feel you need more help, read the 1st 3rd of the passage of the main idea, less if you're comfortable.

3. **The main idea is the most important**. Put the passage in your own words. All correct answer choices are in line with the main idea of the passage.

4. **Read the question, and then answer it BEFORE reading the answer choices**. Remember, the answer choices are not your friends. They are there to trap you. If you know what you are looking for 1st, then you can eliminate what doesn't work.

5. **Eliminate first**. Do not try to hunt for the right answer first. The right one may not look right compared to reasonable traps. By using your paraphrasing and the main idea. You are able to get rid of the wrong ones.

STEPS FOR READING

1

- This primes your brain so you have an idea of what you will be reading.

2

- This contains the main idea. You want enough information to get the gist of what is going on. As you skim, think of these two questions:

    >> **What am I reading?** Note what the passage is discussing.

    >> **Why am I reading this?** No, not because you have to. Your answer should include what message the author is trying to send. Try to pick up any emotions or opinions the author expresses.

ANSWERING QUESTIONS

1

There are three main types of questions:

>> Vocabulary-in-context

>> Line Reference

>> Main Idea

They are not arranged in this order but should be answered in this order because of the amount of information needed for each question.

>>> Vocabulary in context <<<

This question needs the least amount of information. It asks how is an author using a certain word. The question contains the phrase "most nearly means." The best way to answer this question is to treat it like a sentence completion. Why? Because most of the answer choices are definitions of the word. You need to figure out, via context, how the word is being used. The best way to do this is to eliminate the word and choose your own word that could replace it.

>> Go to the line in which the word is located. Physically mark out the word, it no longer exists.

>> Read up about 3 lines and sown about 3 lines to give yourself enough context. Predict your answer.

>> Eliminate answer choices that don't work.

>> Choose the best one.

In August, some friends and I were sitting around a
30 nighttime campfire. Our six-person camping group included
one young lawyer. The rest of us were saying that it is wrong
for lawyers to defend clients they know to be guilty. The
lawyer found this claim offensive. Everyone is entitled to the
best defense, she argued. This is the basis of the adversary
35 system of law: justice lies in having advocates of the two
sides make their best case. The American adversary system is
driven not by a search for truth but by a search for the best
defense.

The word "claim" (line 33) most nearly means

(A) requirement
(B) assertion
(C) entitlement
(D) demand
(E) right

Imagining the unseeable is hard, because *imagining*
25 means having an image in your mind. And how can you
have a mental image of something you have never seen?
Like perception itself, the models of science are embed-
ded inextricably in the current worldview we call culture.
Imagine (if you can) what the planetary model of the atom
30 would have looked like, its satellite electrons orbiting its
sunlike nucleus, if people had still thought the Earth was
flat. It would have been literally unthinkable. Unable to
suppose what the universe is really like, we rely on our
rather limited but comfortably familiar models. The look
35 of those models changes periodically, with the result that
our view of the universe changes dramatically. It's a long
way from Newton's mechanical universe to today's images
of forces as wrinkles in space, of matter as mere vibrating
wisps of energy, of the physical world we know as but a
40 shadow of a higher eleven-dimensional reality. "Scientific

In line 33, "suppose" most nearly means

(A) pretend
(B) imply
(C) believe
(D) conceive
(E) anticipate

>>> Line Reference <<<

Most of the questions are this type. The question gives you several lines of information and tests your understanding.

>> Go back to the line reference in the passage.

>> Read up 3 lines and down 3 lines, give or take a line to finish a sentence. The answer is not in the line reference itself, but it is in the relationship with the surrounding information.

>> Paraphrase your answer before looking at the answer choices. Your paraphrasing does not have to be perfect. Even if the only thing you can do is rephrase the passage of jot down a phrase that you understand. You have enough to eliminate what you can.

>> Eliminate what doesn't match. You are not looking for what you like or can rationalize. Use your paraphrasing (write it down if you have to) and the main idea to get rid of what won't work.

>> Choose the best answer. Once you have eliminated most of the answer choices, you should be able to point to the passage and prove why it's the best one.

"Marta del Angel" from "Americas Review" by Linda Macias Feyder is reprinted with permission from the publisher (1991 Arte Publico Press-University of Houston)

Questions 28-35 are based on the following passage.

This passage was adapted from a 1998 book written by a social scientist who is an expert on miscommunication.

We look to courts to reveal the truth, and often they do. But the United States legal system isn't designed to uncover truth – at least not directly. It's about winning. The American legal system is a prime example of trying to
5 solve problems by pitting two sides against each other and letting them slug it out in public. It reflects and reinforces our assumption that truth emerges when two polarized, warring extremes are set against each other.

The United States has a long and proud tradition of
10 using the law to bring about social change (in the Civil Rights movement, for example) and exposing wrong-doing (for example, that tobacco companies knew about and concealed the link between smoking and lung cancer). We regard the law as a cherished route to truth and justice,
15 and it often leads us there.

But just as some journalists are expressing concern about developments in their profession, some lawyers are expressing concern about theirs. The District of Columbia Bar and the New York State Court of Appeals have
20 recommended or adopted codes to curb overly aggressive strategies commonly referred to as "pit bull" or "scorched earth" tactics. Many complaints address abuses of the system. And some are questioning the system itself, especially its adversary character. Lawsuits are
25 adversarial by nature. But the United States system of law is more adversarial than others, and some in the legal profession believe that its adversary structure causes problems at the same time that it attempts to solve them.

In August, some friends and I were sitting around a
30 nighttime campfire. Our six-person camping group included one young lawyer. The rest of us were saying that it is wrong for lawyers to defend clients they know to be guilty. The lawyer found this claim offensive. Everyone is entitled to the best defense, she argued. This is the basis of the adversary
35 system of law: justice lies in having advocates of the two sides make their best case. The American adversary system is driven not by a search for truth but by a search for the best defense.

Nothing can be more partisan than our legal system,
40 in which facts are uncovered and revealed by lawyers who are advocates for the two parties in dispute. How else could it be? In the German and French systems, fact gathering is controlled by a judge, not by attorneys. The judge does most of the questioning of witnesses, and the judge's goal
45 is to determine what happened, as nearly as possible. Such a system surely has its own liabilities, but it provides an illuminating contrast to the goal of attorneys in the adversary system: to manipulate facts to the advantage of their side.

A leading critic of the adversary system is Carrie
50 Menkel-Meadow, professor of law at Georgetown University. She shows many ways that the adversary system fails to serve us well even if there is no miscarriage of justice. For one thing, it encourages lawyers to overstate claims, puffing up their side to persuade. This gets in
55 the way of the truth coming out. For another, there has been a rash of complaints against attorneys who suppress evidence. This, Menkel-Meadow maintains, is the inevitable result of requiring lawyers to do everything they can to win for their client. Yet another weakness goes to
60 the heart of the system: in many civil disputes there is some right on both sides. In those cases, a winner-take-all result cannot be fair, yet that is the type of resolution the system is designed to seek.

Menkel-Meadow illustrates another way the adversary
65 system can obstruct justice. Those who recoil from open conflict – whether because of cultural experience, individual temperament, or simply a realistic appreciation of the toll it takes to be involved in a lawsuit – do not get relief for injustice. Perhaps most important, Menkel-
70 Meadow says, many people who pass through our legal system emerge bitter and angry, and this is dangerous for society, which depends upon the trust of its citizens for the institutions making up that society to work.

The reference to the "District of Columbia Bar and the New York State Court of Appeals" (lines 18-19) serves to

(A) illustrate attempts to reduce the severity of a problem

(B) emphasize the prestige of two powerful legal entities

(C) highlight the close ties between the court system and bar associations

(D) call into question the integrity of two legal institutions

(E) underscore how the quest to win has eclipsed the search for truth

Lines 48-49 ("to manipulate...side") refer to what the author most likely believes to be

(A) a universal approach

(B) a baffling phenomenon

(C) a troubling practice

(D) an unorthodox strategy

(E) an unanticipated consequence

Menkel-Meadow's argument in lines 70-73 suggests most directly that if the American legal system continues unchanged, then

(A) judges will need to take over some of the roles of attorneys

(B) lawyers will become more interested in collecting fees than winning cases

(C) numerous citizens will lose confidence in a central social institution

(D) advocates for judicial reform will intensify their efforts

(E) the German and French systems will gain adherents around the world

>>> Tone Practice Question <<<

Which of the following best describes how the young lawyer felt about what "The rest of us were saying" (line 31)?

(A) Disgusted

(B) Embarrassed

(C) Vindictive

(D) Disillusioned

(E) Affronted

>>> Main Idea/Tone <<<

The last type of question requires your understanding of the whole passage. After you have answered most of the questions, recall the running theme of the passage, the message that the author repeated throughout. Tone questions ask you to understand the emotions, thoughts, and opinions. Think about any descriptive information that will lead you to a positive, negative, neutral or scholarly tone.

>> Reread the 1ˢᵗ 3ʳᵈ if needed.

>> Use what you know about the passage discussed and the main idea you figured out at the beginning.

>> Eliminate answer choices.

>> Choose the one you can prove from the passage.

>>> Main Idea Practice <<<

From the previous passage...

The passage suggests that compared to the American system, the German and French legal systems would be

(A) more likely to resolve disputes expeditiously

(B) as likely to entail wrangling over procedure

(C) as likely to infringe on the rights of the accused

(D) less likely to provide court-appointed counsel

(E) less likely to encourage distortion of the facts

The passage is best described as

(A) an endorsement of strict ethical standards for lawyers

(B) an inquiry into the abuses of clients' trust committed by lawyers

(C) a proposal for eliminating needless lawsuits

(D) a criticism of the basic structure of the United States legal system

(E) a historical account of the development of jurisprudence in the United

    States

" The best way to handle the questions is to eliminate what is wrong. Luckily, the traps, along with their temptations, give clues to the wrong info they contain. "

>>> Types of Wrong Answer Choices <<<

>> Extreme or absolute language

>> Politically incorrect choices

>> Choices the defy common sense

>> Choices that go beyond the scope of the passage

>> Rational ones that don't answer the question

>> Pointless

>> Contradict the passage or line reference

>>> IMPORTANT NOTE <<<

Except/Least/Not – these types of questions won't necessarily allow you to follow the strategies. You do have to read through the choices to eliminate what DOES work.

DIFFICULT PASSAGES

The passages on the SAT are not meant to be a piece of cake. The subject matter is usually boring or complex and will more than likely be unfamiliar. Don't worry, using the strategies listed above, you should be able to tackle the questions.

However, there are a couple of passages that tend to be more difficult: **Narrative** and **Science**.

Why are they so hard ?

Narrative passages are usually challenging because of their structure. Narratives are stories about characters and their emotions, thoughts, and interactions with others.

During a timed, stressful situation, it is often difficult to gather the pieces of information needed. Most of these passages' questions will revolve around you having to infer the relationships, motives, and feelings of the characters.

>>> How to handle narrative passages <<<

>> **Pay attention to the characters.** Use the words the author uses to describe the characters, their conversations, thoughts, and emotions, which all give clues to their personalities and motives for their actions.

>> **Focus on the point of the story.** Ask yourself "What is the point?" or "Why is the author telling me this?"

Why are they so hard ?

Science passages are difficult simply because their content is usually hard to understand. What you have to know is you are not required to know everything about the topic well enough to explain it to others.

Don't let unfamiliar vocabulary or confusing details get in the way. Here is how you attack these passages:

>>> How to handle science passages <<<

>> **Don't sweat the details.** You need a main idea to help you eliminate answer choices. If you run into a difficult detail or word you just can't make out, don't dwell on it. Focus on what you do know.

>> **Use the organization to your advantage.** The Science passage is usually the most organized. The first sentence tells you what the passage's topic is and the rest of this paragraph gives the main idea. The first sentence of the subsequent paragraphs is the main ideas of those paragraphs. Review those as necessary. Finally, the last paragraph is usually a summary of the passage. This is also very helpful for further information.

>> **Find the answer in the passage.** Since these are factual, review the passage and then paraphrase your findings.

DOUBLE PASSAGES

Don't worry because **there's never more than two** in an entire test.

The Double passages are two passages about the same topic, yet are written by different authors that have different opinions. To answer these questions:

>>> How to handle double passages <<<

>> Follow the steps for passage 1

>> Follow the steps for passage 2

>> Attack the Compare/Contrast questions

These two passages are adapted from books written in 2003 and 2004, respectively.

Passage 1

It is easy to understand why the mind may appear to be a forbidding, unapproachable mystery. The mind, as an entity, seems to be different in kind from other things we know, namely, from the objects around
5 us and from the parts of our own bodies that we see and touch. One view says that the body and its parts are physical matter while the mind is not. On one side is the physically extensive matter that constitutes the cells, tissues, and organs of our bodies. On the other side is the
10 stuff we cannot touch – all the rapidly formed feelings, sights, and sounds that make up the thoughts in our minds. This view is no longer mainstream in science or philosophy, although it is probably the view that most human beings today would regard as their own.
15 This idea of the dualism of the mind and the body was dignified by seventeenth-century philosopher and scientist Rene' Descartes. Descartes also proposed that the mind and the body interacted, yet he never explained how the interaction might take place beyond
20 saying that the pineal gland was the conduit for such interactions. The pineal is a small structure, located at the midline and base of the brain, and it turns out to be rather poorly connected and endowed for the momentous job Descartes required of it.

25 Whether Descartes really believed in mind-body dualism is by no means certain. He might have believed it at some point and then not, which is not meant at all as a criticism. It would simply mean Descartes was uncertain and ambivalent about a problem
30 that has chronically plunged human beings into precisely the same state of uncertainty and ambivalence. Very human and very understandable.
In spite of its scientific shortcomings, the view identified with Descartes resonates well with the awe
35 and wonder we deservedly have for our minds. There is no doubt that the human mind is special – special in its immense capacity to feel pleasure and pain and to be aware of the pain and pleasure of others; in its ability to symbolize and narrate; in its gift of language with
40 syntax; in its power to understand the universe and create new universes; in the speed and ease with which it processes and integrates disparate information so that problems can be solved. But awe and wonder at the human mind are compatible with other views of the
45 relation between the body and the mind and do not make Descartes' views any more correct.

Passage 2

It is popular in some quarters to claim that the human brain is largely unstructured at birth; it is tempting to believe that our minds float free of our
50 genomes.* But such beliefs are completely at odds with everything that scientists have learned in molecular biology over the past decade. From cell division to cell differentiation, every process that is used in the development of the body is also used in the development
55 of the brain.

The idea that the brain might be assembled in much the same way as the rest of the body – on the basis of the action of thousands of autonomous but interacting genes – is anathema to our deeply held feelings that our
60 minds are special, somehow separate from the material world. Yet at the same time, for the Western intellectual tradition, it is a continuation, perhaps the culmination, of a growing up for the human species that for too long has overestimated its own centrality in the universe.
65 Copernicus showed us that our planet is not at the center of the universe. William Harvey showed that our heart is a mechanical pump. John Dalton and the nineteenth-century chemists showed that our bodies are, like all other matter, made up of atoms. Watson and Crick
70 showed us how genes emerge from chains of carbon, hydrogen, oxygen, nitrogen, and phosphorus. In the 1990s, the Decade of the Brain, cognitive neuroscientists showed that our minds are the product of our brains. Early returns from this century are showing that the
75 mechanisms that build our brains are just a special case of the mechanisms that build the rest of our bodies. The initial structure of the mind, like the initial structure of the rest of the body, is a product of our genes.

Although some might see the idea that our
80 brains are just a bunch of molecules, grown in all the usual ways, as a bleak renunciation of all that is special about humanity, to me it is an exciting modern take on an old idea, there is a bond that unifies all living things. Through advances in molecular biology and
85 neuroscience, we can now understand better than ever just how deeply we share our biological make-up – physical and mental – with all the creatures with which we share our planet.

*genomes: the genetic material of an organism

1. The tone of the comment that closes the third paragraph of Passage 1 (lines 31-32) is best described as

   (A) sarcastic
   (B) apologetic
   (C) impartial
   (D) admiring
   (E) sympathetic

2. With which statement regarding the view described in lines 6-7 of Passage 1 ("One…not") would the author of Passage 2 most likely agree?

   (A) It has been undermined by recent discoveries in molecular biology.
   (B) It has been strengthened by modern ideas about humans' place in the universe.
   (C) It is supported by cognitive neuroscientists.
   (D) It is promoted by contemporary philosophers.
   (E) It is consistent with the findings of nineteenth-century chemists.

3. The author of Passage 2 would most likely view the attitude described in lines 34-36, Passage 1 ("the awe… is special"), as an example of the tendency of humans to

   (A) dispute scientific advances
   (B) defend their own skepticism
   (C) exaggerate the role of the body
   (D) overemphasize their distinctiveness
   (E) resist identifying with other people

4. Both passages suggest that the notion that the mind and body are separate is

   (A) appealing but problematic
   (B) novel but impractical
   (C) rational and reassuring
   (D) innovative and controversial
   (E) demeaning and shortsighted

5. In line 36, Passage 1, and line 60, Passage 2, the word "special" most nearly means

   (A) primary
   (B) additional
   (C) exceptional
   (D) definite
   (E) featured

6. Which best describes the final sentences of Passage 1 (lines 43-46) and Passage 2 (lines 84-88), respectively?

   (A) Perplexed…resigned
   (B) Cautionary…stirring
   (C) Ironic…dismissive
   (D) Reverent…dispassionate
   (E) Indignant…surprised

SMALL PASSAGES

After the sentence completions, there are two paragraphs with two questions a piece. For these passages, you will have to read the paragraph, paying particular attention to the first and last sentences. These two sentences provide you with the main idea of the passage. Remember, the main idea is a key piece of information needed to answer the questions.

>>> How to handle small passages <<<

>> **Read the passage, paying attention to the first and last sentences**

>> **Title the passage**
  > Your title doesn't need to be overly long, just 3 or 4 words letting you know the main point

>> **Read the question and refer back to the passage for the answer**

>> **Predict your answer**

>> **Eliminate answer choices and choose the best one**

Short Passages

Every now and again, cosmologists decide that the universe needs "redecorating." Sometimes they declutter, as when Copernicus shuffled the Sun and the Earth to make the planets move in a straightforward
5 orbits. Sometimes they embellish, as when Einstein decided there's more to space than good old-fashioned nothingness and introduced the concept of a deformable space-time. They're at it again. But this time it's different. Like the decorator who strips away
10 wallpaper to reveal a crumbling wall, cosmologists are realizing that their discovery that something is speeding up the expansion of the universe points to serious problems with their models. When they're done fixing things, chances are we'll hardly recognize the place.

Charles Chesnutt, one of the first critically-acclaimed African American writers, was born in 1858. His stories display a keen ear for language and understanding of both the tragedy of slavery and the
5 heartbreak of Reconstruction. Chesnutt earned immediate accolades as a creator of "fresh, vivid, dramatic sketches" in a "new and delightful vein." He shared with other writers such as Bret Harte an intensity of feeling for the rawness of an emergent
10 America. Chesnutt portrayed human loss and torment - sometimes with pathos, but more often with a wit like an ax cutting into a tree in the backwoods of the North Carolina he knew so well.

The author uses "declutter" (line 3), "embellish" (line 5), and "fixing" (line 13) to

(A) establish a tone of breezy disdain
(B) emphasize the complexity of an issue
(C) vary the terms of a critique
(D) expand upon an earlier figure of speech
(E) explain the details of a technical theory

The quotations in lines 6-7 serve as examples of

(A) the reactions of some of Chesnutt's contemporaries to his stories
(B) Chesnutt's pronouncements about the purpose of fiction writing
(C) the type of language that appears in Chesnutt's stories
(D) the shared language of nineteenth-century short-story writers
(E) the unintelligible jargon of modern-day literary critics

The last sentence of the passage ("When...place") implies that the

(A) recent views of the cosmos are aesthetically satisfying
(B) current cosmological methods can be bewilderingly complex
(C) new breed of cosmologist will do unnecessary damage
(D) contemporary astronomical theories will be thoroughly tested by the scientific community
(E) current cosmological research will transform our understanding of the universe

The description in lines 11-13 ("more...well") suggests that many of Chesnutt's stories

(A) are more realistic than those written by Bret Harte
(B) evoke a warm and sentimental response
(C) influenced the writings of other African American authors
(D) are both forceful and penetrating in their insights
(E) offer vivid depictions of life in the North Carolina wilderness

TURN THE TABLES ON THE TEST-MAKERS

SAT / ACT

Writing

WRITING

BREAKDOWN...

The writing section of the SAT is composed of 2 multiple choice sections and an essay. The multiple choice sections contain 49 questions (a section of 35 and a section of 14). The multiple choice questions test your understanding of standardized written English.

ESSAY (25 Minutes)

Section I (25 Minutes)

Improving Sentences	Questions 1-11
Identifying Error	Questions 12-29
Improving the Paragraphs	Questions 30-35

Section II (20 Minutes)

Improving Sentences	Questions 1-8

**Each Improving Sentences and Identifying the Error section is loosely organized from easy to hard.

Why are they so hard   ?

>> First, most students haven't been taught grammar since the 8th grade. Many rules have been forgotten over the years, so it is difficult to remember how to use those rules.

>> Second, the questions require you to use your editing skills, skills rarely implemented regularly. Once you realize that the test makers are testing your knowledge of written rules, this section will be much easier.

TYPES OF QUESTIONS

>> **Improving Sentence Questions (25 total)**

These sentences have an underlined portion that may or may not contain errors. Answer choice (A) is the same as the original, so treat it as NO CHANGE.

>> **Identifying Sentence Errors (18 total)**

Each sentence has 4 underlined portions, of which one may be incorrect. There is also an option (E), which is NO CHANGE.

>> **Improving Paragraphs (6 total)**

You will have a passage structured to mimic a first draft of a short essay. The types of question for the passage cover grammar, usage, and style errors.

TERMS TO KNOW

Noun	
Pronoun	
Verb	
Adjective	
Adverb	
Conjunction	
Preposition	
Phrase	
Clause	
> Dependent	
> Independent	

STRATEGY FOR ANSWERING

>> Know what to look for

Understanding the types of errors you will encounter is key to mastering the writing section. Errors will be discussed later.

>> Turn off your ear

Using the technique of choosing what "sounds right" will not be in your best interest. Many of the questions contain errors that may not be obvious or questions that do not sound right to your ears but are actually correct.

>> Read Actively

As you read the questions, you should be looking for errors. Ask yourself, "Is there something wrong?"

Turn the Table Techniques

1. "Being" is usually wrong.

2. Be wary of answer choices that change the tense of the verb, especially to the continuous tense (ing), unless there is an error with the tense written.

3. Answer choices that change the meaning of the original sentence are incorrect.

4. Active voice is always better.

5. If you are down between two correctly written answer choices, choose the one that is shorter.

6. About 20% of the sentences will be correctly written. Don't be afraid to select NO CHANGE.

ERRORS TO LOOK FOR

PRONOUNS

>> Number Agreement

- Nouns and pronouns used in the same sentence or thought must agree in number, singular nouns need singular pronouns and plural nouns need plural pronouns. Errors happen when the pronoun does not agree with its antecedent.

>> Contractions

- Contractions are two words that are connected with an apostrophe to create one word. **Errors occur when either the possessive from is used instead of the contraction or vice versa.** A simple rule to remember is pronoun possessives DO NOT have apostrophes.

>> Ambiguity

- The SAT does not want you to assume you know what a sentence means. Again, the SAT is very literal. Ambiguous pronouns leave you unsure about their true antecedents.

Subject/Object/Possessive Chart

Subject: Actor in the sentence	Object: Receiver of the action	Possessive: Owner in the sentence	
I	Me	**Adjective:** used before a noun	**Pronoun:** used alone
You	You	My	Mine
He, She, It	Him, Her, It	Your	Yours
We	Us	His, Her, Its	His, Hers, Its
They	Them	Our	Ours
		Thiers	Theirs

Pronoun Practice

>> In the first two, circle what you think is wrong, if anything:

When the <u>women's</u> shelter began <u>to publish</u> an electronic newsletter instead of a written one,

<u>they</u> brought a new awareness to this simple yet <u>powerful</u> environmental course of action.

<u>No error</u>

<u>During</u> the last <u>part of</u> the competition, the opposing team <u>forfeited</u>, making <u>Jane and I</u> the

winners. <u>No error</u>

>> Now try to improve this one (Remember, choice (A) will be the same):

The choir's spirited singing and choreographed <u>dancing made them the obvious</u>

<u>choice for the judges</u>.

(A) dancing made them the obvious choice for the judges.

(B) dancing made them the obvious choices for the judges.

(C) dances caused the judges to view them as the obvious choices.

(D) dancing made it the obvious choice for the judges.

(E) dancing making it the obvious choice for the judges.

SUBJECT/VERB AGREEMENT

- One of the foundations of good writing is subject/verb agreement. Anytime a sentence has a verb underlined, figure out the true subject of the sentence and make sure they agree in number.

- **A simple rule that helps many English as Second Language students learn the difference between singular and plural verbs is that singular verbs have an "s" on the end of them.**

- To make these questions difficult, the SAT writers separate the true subject from its verb by including unnecessary information between them or by inverting the order of the sentence, making the verb appear first.

- Similar to pronoun agreement errors, sentences will contain collective nouns that may sound plural. Don't fall for the trap!

Subject/Verb Practice

>> In the first two, circle what you think is wrong, if anything:

Organs located in the tail of the electric eel enables the animal to produce electricity, which it uses in hunting prey. No error

Hanging on the wall of her office is Mindy's diplomas from the undergraduate and graduate universities she attended. No error

>> Now try to improve this one (Remember, choice (A) will be the same):

As freshman year continues, the balance between academics and socializing become more important, challenging, and frightening for first-year students.

(A) become more important, challenging, and frightening for first-year students.

(B) when it becomes important, challenging, and it can frighten.

(C) becomes more important, challenging, and frightening for first-year students.

(D) becoming more important, challenging, and frightening for first-year students.

(E) becomes most important, challenging, and frightening to those first-year students.

MODIFICATION

- Modifying phrases are used to describe other parts of a sentence. A rule for modifying phrases is they must be next to whatever they are describing. If they aren't, the sentence must be changed.

Modification Practice

In collaboration with her mother, a fashion designer, *Echoes of Harlem* was produced by the artist Faith Ringgold, the first of her large, painted story quilts, in 1980.

    (A) *Echoes of Harlem* was produced by the artist Faith Ringgold,

    (B) *Echoes of Harlem*, produced by the artist Faith Ringgold as

    (C) the artist Faith Ringgold produced *Echoes of Harlem*,

    (D) the artist Faith Ringgold having produced *Echoes of Harlem* as

    (E) the artist Faith Ringgold producing *Echoes of Harlem*

In order to gain a deeper understanding of the behavior of chimpanzees and other primates, a 45-year study of chimpanzee social and family life conducted by primatologist Jane Goodall.

    (A) a 45-year study of chimpanzee social and family life conducted by primatologist Jane Goodall.

    (B) a 45-year study of chimpanzee social and family life that was conducted by primatologist Jane Goodall.

    (C) primatologist Jane Goodall who conducted a 45-year stud of chimpanzee social and family life.

    (D) therefore primatologist Jane Goodall conducts a 45-year study of chimpanzee social and family life.

    (E) primatologist Jane Goodall conducted a 45-year study of chimpanzee social and family life.

Realizing that her brother had not eaten for hours, ingredients were bought by her to cook a large dinner.

    (A) ingredients were bought by her to cook

    (B) ingredients were bought to cook

    (C) she bought ingredients to cook

    (D) she bought ingredients in the preparation to cook

    (E) she had bought ingredients to cook

PARALLELISM

- Parallelism ensures all parts of the sentence are written in a consistent manner. Be on the lookout for lists of items and make sure they are in the same form.

Parallelism Practice

The Piraha people of Brazil <u>communicate</u> almost as much by singing, whistling, <u>and</u> humming <u>than</u> they do by <u>pronouncing</u> consonants and vowels. <u>No error</u>

Everyone can help reduce environmental pollution by traveling on public transportation whenever possible, choosing low-toxicity paints, and <u>if fewer household chemical products are used.</u>

(A) if fewer household chemical products are used.

(B) if they use fewer household chemical products.

(C) if one uses fewer household chemical products.

(D) the use of fewer household chemical products.

(E) using fewer household chemical products.

COMPARISONS

- Items being compared need to be the same. You can only compare books to books or people to people.

- You must also be careful of the adjectives used to compare things. If the sentence is comparing two things, the sentence must use "more" or add "er" to the end of the adjective. Sentences comparing three or more things must use "most" or add "est" to words.

Comparisons Practice

In response to <u>increasing global competition</u>, the company <u>has pledged</u> to provide professional development programs to ensure that <u>its</u> employees are the most <u>highest qualified</u> in the field. <u>No error</u>

<u>Unlike the bustling city of Anchorage where it begins,</u> the Iditarod dogsled race runs through vast tracts of wilderness separating small towns and villages.

    (A) Unlike the bustling city of Anchorage where it begins,

    (B) Contrary to beginning in the bustling city of Anchorage,

    (C) It begins in the bustling city of Anchorage, however,

    (D) Beginning in the bustling city of Anchorage, but

    (E) Though it begins in the bustling city of Anchorage,

<u>Nearly all</u> of the food critics <u>agree</u> that <u>of the chef's</u> three signature dishes, the lamb is the <u>more</u> delectable. <u>No error</u>

VERB TENSES

- Verb tenses need to stay consistent unless the meaning of the sentence warrants a change.

  The following are the main tenses and their usages:
  - \>\> **Present** – expresses an action or state of being that is a routine or fact
  - \>\> **Past** – expresses action or state of being that occurred in the past
  - \>\> **Future** – expresses an action or state of being that will occur in the future
  - \>\> **Continuous (ing)** – expresses an action or state of being that is occurring at the moment (most actions on the test do not occur in this tense)

- Along with these main tenses, there are two other tenses that you need to understand.

  - \>\> **Present Perfect** – formed using has or have and the past participle of a verb. This tense is used in two situations
    1. Actions that began in the past and continue currently
    2. Actions that occurred at an unspecified point in the past

  - \>\> **Past Perfect** – formed using had and the past participle of a verb. Used to express the relationship between two past tense actions, one that happened before the other.

When he finished reading the story of King Dushyanta and the young maiden Shakuntala, the director <u>has decided</u> to make the classic Indian tale into a movie.

    (A) has decided

    (B) having decided

    (C) deciding

    (D) will decide

    (E) decided

<u>Elected</u> president of the United Nations General Assembly in 1953, Indian diplomat Vijaya Lakshmi Pandit <u>had rose</u> to political prominence <u>during</u> India's struggle for <u>independence from</u> Great Britain. <u>No error</u>

Flying buttresses, like those used in the construction of the Gothic cathedral at Chartres, France, <u>had relieved pressure on a building's walls by transmitting</u> the roof's thrust outward to exterior pillars.

    (A) had relieved pressure on a building's walls by transmitting

    (B) relieves pressures on a building's walls, it transmits

    (C) relieving pressure on a building's walls by transmitting

    (D) relieve pressure on a building's walls by transmitting

    (E) by relieving pressure on a building's walls and transmit

PREPOSITIONAL IDIOMS

- Idioms are not based on grammar rules, they are simply phrases that have a special meaning when used together. Since they are not based on specific rules, the phrases must be memorized.

- Linking expressions – also called correlative conjunctions are also on the test. When you see one, you must use the other.
  >> Examples: either/or, neither/nor, not only/but (also), whether/or

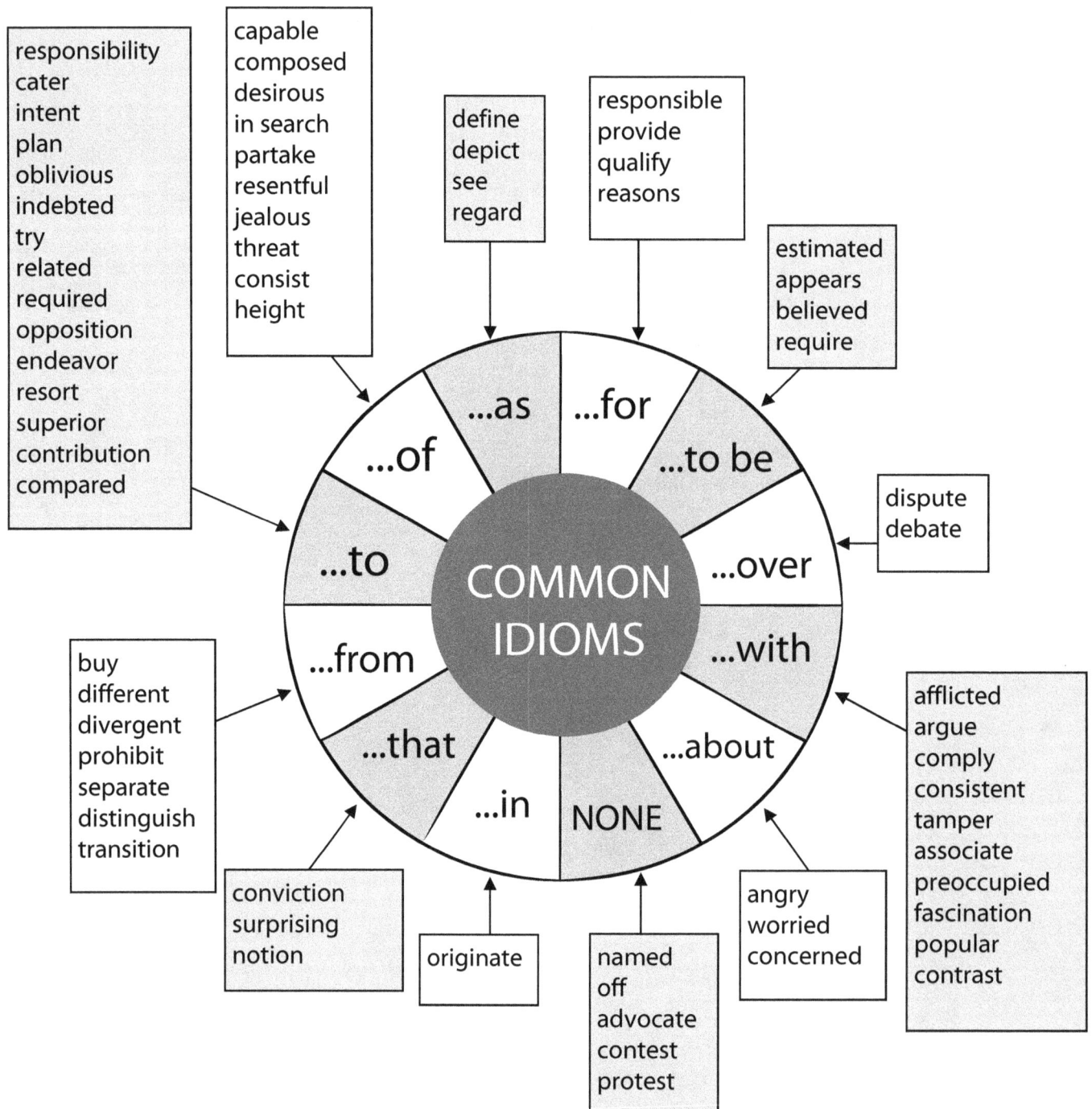

responsibility
cater
intent
plan
oblivious
indebted
try
related
required
opposition
endeavor
resort
superior
contribution
compared

capable
composed
desirous
in search
partake
resentful
jealous
threat
consist
height

define
depict
see
regard

responsible
provide
qualify
reasons

estimated
appears
believed
require

dispute
debate

afflicted
argue
comply
consistent
tamper
associate
preoccupied
fascination
popular
contrast

buy
different
divergent
prohibit
separate
distinguish
transition

conviction
surprising
notion

originate

named
off
advocate
contest
protest

angry
worried
concerned

COMMON IDIOMS

...as

...for

...of

...to be

...to

...over

...from

...with

...that

...about

...in

NONE

The Voting Rights Act prohibits <u>states to use</u> literacy tests to keep citizens from voting.

    (A) states to use

    (B) that states not use

    (C) against states using

    (D) states from using

    (E) states to the use of

Frances Harper <u>won fame</u> not only <u>for her poems</u> opposing slavery <u>and also</u> for her lectures <u>supporting</u> women's suffrage. <u>No error</u>

<u>Last week</u>, the local department store lowered <u>its</u> prices as a way <u>at attracting</u> a larger number of customers <u>during</u> the holiday season. <u>No error</u>

SENTENCE STRUCTURE

>> RUN-ON
- Run-on sentences occur when two or more independent thoughts are connected improperly. There are 3 ways to correct them:
    1. Semi-colon
    2. Comma and a conjunction (For, And, Nor, But, Or, Yet, So)
    3. Period (this way will not be a common option)

>> FRAGMENT
- Fragments occur when a sentence doesn't include a complete thought. Oftentimes, the use of the continuous tense of a verb causes the error.

Sentence Structure Practice

Ernest Withers, who with his camera famously documented the Civil Rights Movement of the 1950s and <u>1960s, he also photographed</u> such baseball icons as Jackie Robinson and Willie Mays.

    (A) 1960s, he also photographed

    (B) 1960s, and photographer of

    (C) 1960s, also photographed

    (D) 1960s as well as photographing

    (E) 1960s and photographed

Learning a new language is common among international students, the majority <u>of them need</u> proficiency in English to advance their studies.

    (A) of them need

    (B) need

    (C) of them are needing

    (D) of which need

    (E) of whom need

The devastating impact of <u>many diseases, often unchecked in developing nations because</u> education and information are difficult to spread.

    (A) many diseases, often unchecked in developing nations because

    (B) many diseases is often unchecked in developing nations and

    (C) many diseases is often unchecked in developing nations where

    (D) many diseases, often unchecked in developing nations and

    (E) many diseases, often unchecked in developing nations when

ADJECTIVES/ADVERBS

- Adjectives describe nouns and pronouns. Adverbs describe verbs, adjectives, and other adverbs. Make certain that when one of these words is underlined, it is modifying the correct word or phrase.

Adverb/Adjective Practice

The dance team <u>in the competition</u> <u>clearly</u> expected to hear <u>loudly</u> clapping during <u>its</u> bows. <u>No error</u>

A relationship <u>between</u> therapist and patient <u>promotes</u> healing <u>more quick</u> than when a therapist simply tells a patient how <u>to feel</u>. <u>No error</u>

WORDINESS

- While not a grammar rule, on the SAT, shorter sentences are always the better choices out of two correct choices.

Wordiness Practice

<u>By exercising vigorously for at least 30 minutes every day</u>, it can lower levels of bad cholesterol by as much as 30 percent.

    (A) By exercising vigorously for at least 30 minutes every day, it
    (B) If one exercises vigorously for at least 30 minutes every day, it
    (C) Exercising vigorously for at least 30 minutes every day
    (D) If you exercise vigorously for at least 30 minutes every day, one
    (E) To exercise vigorous for at least 30 minutes every day

According to legend, <u>the country of Vietnam was created when the Princess of the Mountains was united with the King of the Sea</u>, a nation known for its beautiful mountains and scenic coasts.

    (A) the country of Vietnam was created when the Princess of the Mountains was united with the King of the Sea
    (B) the country of Vietnam being created when the Princess of the mountains was united with the King of the Sea
    (C) when the Princess of the Mountains was united with the King of the Sea, they created the country of Vietnam
    (D) the Princess of the Mountains and the King of the Sea united to create the country of Vietnam

DICTION

- Diction refers to word choice. There will be a few questions that will ask you to choose the correct word. These choices are usually commonly misused words.

    >> Consciousness vs. Conscience
    >> Affect vs. Effect
    >> Infer vs. Imply
    >> Compliment vs. Complement
    >> Allusion vs. Illusion

Diction Practice

Hurricanes are <u>such an intent</u> threat to the area that it <u>is</u> imperative that the local community <u>find</u> new ways <u>to predict</u> them. <u>No error</u>

<u>With</u> the help of an enormous truck, the construction company employee <u>rose</u> the new structural bridge <u>on</u> <u>the</u> corner <u>across from</u> the church. <u>No error</u>

THE ESSAY

- The essay is the first section of the SAT. You will be presented with a prompt and will have 25 minutes to write an effective, cogent essay.

- Two graders will read your essay and assign it a score of 1 to 6, which will then be added together for a score of 2 to 12. The essay accounts for 30% of your Writing score.

- Readers grade your essay holistically, meaning they do not grade you on specific elements but on the overall impression they get from your writing.

What the Readers Expect to See

>> A Well organized essay

- Easy to read
- Transitions that connect ideas logically
- Examples that are related to the prompt

>> Well developed, complex ideas

- Examples are descriptive and thought out
- Specific topics and not vague generalities
- Ideas are expressed in an interesting manner

>> Effective use of language

- Few, if any, grammar errors
- Varied sentence structure
- Higher-level vocabulary

"You should not worry about the readers liking your examples.

HOW you present your material is more important than WHAT material you present. However, you should prepare a list of examples ahead of time. "

Examples of some examples

>> Literature
Most books read in school cover a vast array of topics and can be applied to many different prompts. This list should give you some ideas, but it is in no way an exhaustive list.

The Scarlet Letter, To Kill a Mockingbird, The Great Gatsby, The Crucible, All the Pretty Horses, Beowulf, many of the works by Shakespeare, and short stories.

>> History
Many of the topics discussed in your history classes are all great for the use of facts related to your stance. The following are important moments and people that you can use.

American Revolution, French Revolution, WWI, WWII, The Civil War, Industrial Revolution, Julius Caesar, Martin Luther King Jr., Rosa Parks, John F. Kennedy Jr., and Abraham Lincoln.

>> Current Events
Using current events are a great way to showcase your knowledge of important news stories.

>> Personal Experience
Personal experience examples have to be used cautiously. Stay away from trivial topics and focus on meaningful events that led to personal or educational achievements. Again, it is extremely important that you prove why your example supports your position.

ESSAY ORGANIZATION

Graders read essays very quickly, spending no more than a minute on each read through. They will be looking at your organizational, idea presenting, and writing skills. In order to accomplish these tasks, let's look at how your essay should be organized.

>> The Introduction

- The introduction paragraph should start off strongly. You need to hook the reader in immediately. Stay away from clichéd openings ("Many people believe... I believe this prompt means..."). Grab the reader's attention by using a quote, defining words, or using an example that relates to the prompt. Next, state your stance, usually called a thesis statement. Finally, you should end your paragraph by introducing the examples you will be discussing.

>> Body paragraphs

- The number of body paragraphs you will have depends on how many examples you will use. Quality is more important than quantity, 2 or 3 well developed examples are more important than many underdeveloped ones. Be specific about how your examples support your stance. Use names, dates, and facts.

- Also, make sure you transition between your paragraphs. The first sentence of each body paragraph should transition the reader from the previous paragraph to the current one. Next, details that you include should be relevant to the prompt. The readers will more than likely know the details of your examples, so there is no need to give tons of background information. Lastly, your final sentence should explicitly state how your example relates.

>> Conclusion

- By the time you get to the conclusion, you are probably running out of time. But you must leave yourself a few minutes to write a complete conclusion paragraph. Your conclusion should restate your stance in a way that is not repetitive. Also, end your essay by stating how this prompt is important to humanity.

ACT INTRO

THE TEST

QUICK FACTS

What does ACT stand for? _____

How is it different from the SAT?

Scoring: _____   Max Score: _____

Average, not addition of subsections

Number of sections: _____

Length of sections: E _____   M _____   R _____   S_____   W___

Always follows the same order: _____

Includes higher math: _____

Has an extra type of section: _____

● ●

Are there any possible advantages to taking the ACT over the SAT?

_____ (more straightforward)

_____ (more predictable)

_____ (can often eliminate need for

subject tests!!)

What type of student excels on the ACT?

_____

What's the biggest challenge on the ACT?

_____

Important note about "super-scoring":

Schools often do not super-score ACT tests. With the SAT, schools may take the best score from any one section on any test date to "super-score" your tests, giving you the maximum score possible.

With the ACT, they tend to look at the highest composite score for any one test day.

TURN THE TABLES ON THE TEST-MAKERS

SAT
ACT

ACT ENGLISH

ENGLISH

BREAKDOWN...

75 multiple-choice questions based on 5 passages

Each passage has 15 questions

- Each passage has underlined portions that are numbered

- Beside each numbered section, there are 4 answer choices that correspond to a particular question

"Note: The ACT testmakers don't pull the ole switcheroo on you. You can expect straightforward questions with few tricks."

For the ACT English, there are 5 Table Turning Techniques that can give you the power to ace this test.

1
2
3
4
5

" Many students think that there must be an error in every single question. Don't think this way. About 25% of your answers will be "NO CHANGE." Remember, just because something can be changed doesn't mean it should be. "

1 — THINK LIKE AN EDITOR

- The ACT tests your ability to recognize standardized written English. You have to find errors in either grammar and usage or rhetorical strategy. When you read an underlined portion, you must ask yourself, "Is there something wrong?"

2 — TURN OFF YOUR EAR

- Get rid of the phrase, "It sounds right." many of the test questions are written in order to throw you off. Our brains will sometimes automatically correct the error or read over it. Get in the habit of actively searching for errors.

3 — READ ACTIVELY

- High scoring students attack the test questions. What do we mean by this? We mean that these students hunt out errors and mark up the passages. Become engaged in the test in order to eliminate misreading.

4   DO NOT BASE YOUR ANSWERS ON YOUR PREFERENCES

- The test makers are not interested in your opinion. You should not change something in the passage simply because it can be changed. use your knowledge of English rules, not your biases.

5   KNOW THE RULES

- You cannot play a game without knowing the rules. Treat the ACT the same way. This test is very predictable. It will cover the same types of errors. Once you become familiar with what the test makers ask, you will be able to master this section.

RULES OF WRITING

Before we begin reviewing the specific grammar and style errors, we want to introduce you to the four main rules of writing.

Passages should be:

1

- This goes without saying but passages must be correct according to grammar and usage rules.

2

- Thoughts need to be written in complete sentences.

3

- As few words and punctuation marks as possible.

4

- No ambiguity, the passage must state what it intended to state

5

- Thoughts need to be written in complete sentences

ERRORS

1 SUBJECT-VERB AGREEMENT

- You will be tested on subject-verb agreement. Singular nouns and pronouns require singular verbs and plural nouns and pronouns require plural verbs.
- Most of the sentences will be written in ways that will hide the obviousness of the error.
- Whenever there is a verb underlined, immediately locate the subject, which may not always be right next to the verb.

- Singular verbs have an "s" on the end of them.

- Any noun or pronoun that follows a preposistion is **NOT** the subject of the sentence.

2 PRONOUNS

- Pronouns replace nouns in a sentence. The pronouns and nouns must be consistent in number and gender. If they are not, they must be changed.

Let's look at the various ways that pronouns can be used in passages >>>>>>

Turn the Table Techniques for Pronouns Continued...

> >> Who versus Whom

- Who is the subject pronoun, which is the actor of the sentence. Whom is the object pronoun, which receives the action of the sentence.
- To tell the difference: If you can replace who or whom with he or she, use who.
- If you can replace who or whom with him or her, use whom.

> >> Possession / Contraction

- Test makers like to test students on frequently made errors. One of these types of errors deals with using the wrong form of the pronoun.
- It is important to know that pronoun possession does not include an apostrophe.

Here is a guide to pronoun contractions and possession:

Pronoun	Contraction	Possession
It	It's	Its
They	They're	Their
You	You're	Your
He/She	He's/She's	His/Hers
I	I'm	Mine
Who	Who's	Whose
We	We're	Our

VERB TENSE

3

- Test makers will test your ability to recognize the correct tense of the verbs in the sentence.

- Verb tense signals the time frame of the action or state of being in a sentence. The four *main* tenses are the following:

1

2

3

4

These verbs are formed with an –ing are continuous tenses. These verbs indicate that an action is either going on right now (with am, is, are) or a continuous action that happened in the past (with was and were).

While a sentence on the test may use this tense correctly, be wary of changing a tense to the continuous tense.

- The test makers will also throw you a curve ball and include the perfect tenses of verbs. These tenses always use the helping verb to have and are also used to indicate the time frame of an event.

Present Perfect: (has/have plus past participle) indicates an event started in the past and continues now.

>> **I have taught English for six years.**

Past Perfect: (had plus past participle) indicates that a past tense action occurred before another action.

>> **Melissa had flown to Spain before she flew to France.**

Irregular Verbs: Remember the list in elementary school of verbs that were spelled differently in their past participle forms? Well, they're back and the ACT loves to test students on them.

The participle for of the verb is the form it takes when it's paired with the helping verb to have.

Participle Practice

Present	Past	Past Participle
drink	drank	(have) drunk
swim		
undergo		
eat		
run		

4   ADJECTIVES/ADVERBS

- Adjectives modify (describe) nouns and pronouns. Adverbs modify verbs, adjectives, and other adverbs. ***Most* adverbs end in –ly.**

- Comparisons: When you want to compare two things, add an –er or more to the adjectives. **Three or more things call for –est or most.**

5   SENTENCE STRUCTURE

- Many of the questions on the English section test your ability to recognize the difference between independent and dependent thoughts and how to punctuate these thoughts correctly.

An **independent** thought can stand on its own. It must have a subject, a verb, and be a complete thought.

>> **The store closes at 9 p.m.**

A **dependent** thought cannot stand on its own. It is usually missing a subject, a verb, or main idea.

>> **Down the street and to the left.**

>> STRATEGY

When trying to determine if a thought is independent or dependent, always ask yourself - "Does that make sense?" or if the thought leaves you wanting to know more in order for you to be satisfied. Many times, determining a subject and verb is not enough for you to be satisfied with the thought.

- **Most of the questions dealing with sentence structure test punctuation rules.**

>>> Commas (,)

Commas are featured heavily on the ACT. There are several ways to use commas.

>> Connect independent and dependent thoughts.

Ex: During heavy thunderstorms, my dog usually hides under my bed.

>> Connects 2 independent thoughts.

A comma plus one conjunction (for, and, nor, but, or, yet, so) is used to connect 2 independent thoughts.

Ex: Many individuals long for summer to begin, **but** they quickly grow tired of the intense heat the season brings.

>> Separates unnecessary information from the rest of the sentence.

Commas are used to surround unnecessary information. Before using the commas, check to see if the information is vital to the meaning of the sentence. If the meaning of the sentence would stay the same, use the commas.

Ex: Mammals, such as dogs and cows, birth live young.

>> Separate items in a list.

Ex: Mark enjoys baseball, soccer, and football.

> Even though some people feel that the comma before the and is unnecessary, *always* include it in answer choices on the ACT.

>>> Semi-colons (;)

A semi-colon is used to connect 2 independent, related thoughts.

Semi-colon = (comma + conjunction)

>>>

>>> Colons (:)

Most students rarely use colons, and when they do, students use them to introduce lists. On the ACT, however, colons are also used to connect an independent thought to either another independent thought or a dependent thought. **The first thought is independent** and the second is a definition or explanation of the first.

>>>

>>> Dashes (-)

A single dash is used like a colon and a pair of dashes is used like a pair of commas to separate unnecessary information.

>>>

>>> Apostrophe (')

While not used to connect thoughts, the apostrophe should be mentioned along with the other punctuation marks. When attached to nouns, apostrophes show ownership.

>> Singular: Mary's dog, mom's oven

>> Plural: dogs' dishes, parents' home

>> Irregular: children's backpacks, women's watches

NOTE: The ACT won't give you identical punctuation marks that will be equally acceptable.

>>> Transition Words

- Thoughts must be organized in a clear way. The ACT tests your ability to understand the relationship between ideas. In order to use these words correctly, consider the relationship between the ideas and pick accordingly.

Additional Info
Additionally
Moreover
Besides
Along with
For instance
For example
As well

Contrast
Still
Although
On the other hand
However
Otherwise
Even though

Cause & Effect
As a result
Therefore
So
For
As
Because
Thus
Consequently

RHETORICAL

- Thirty-five of the questions on the English section tests rhetorical or style strategies.

>> **Word Choice**

>> **Prepositional Idioms**

>> **Strategy:** the purpose of the text. These ask you the following:

> add text
> delete text
> purpose of the text
> replace text
> determine the impact of the text

These questions are very literal. Do not think about what the text should be saying, the text needs to state exactly what the answer choice says it's stating.

>> **Order**

Ideas need to logically flow into one another. Look for introductions, pronouns, and transition words. These are clues that let you know if ideas are in their correct order.

If the passage you're working on has sentences that may need reordering, the sentences will be numbered. If there is a question about the order of the paragraphs, there will be a warning at the beginning of the passage.

>> **Writer's goal**

At the end of most passages, there is a question that asks if the writer wrote about what he or she intended to write about. There are two "yes" answers and two "no" answers. You must think about what information was included before deciding if the answer choice matches the content of the passage.

TURN THE TABLES ON THE TEST-MAKERS

ACT MATH

MATH

BREAKDOWN...

The ACT takes math to the next level in a few ways.

- It's longer—Sure, there's only **one** section, but it lasts **60 minutes** and has **60 questions.**
- It incorporates higher math—Get ready to see some **precalculus**.
- There aren't as many tricks—Yes, you can plug in here and there, but not as often as the SAT.

We're going to introduce you to the most common higher-level math you're going to see on the ACT.

● ●

- Logs are weird, but they're really just another way of writing exponents. The easiest way to handle them is to remember:

Left-Right-Center

$$\log_a b = x$$

What letter is on the left? _____
What letter is on the right? _____
What letter is in the center? _____

Cool. Let's rearrange those into another format that looks like this:

$$\text{Left}^{\text{Right}} = \text{Center}$$

Try it with some real numbers:

$\log_8 64 = 2$ _____
$\log_4 64 = 3$ _____

You can also go backwards!

$6^3 = 216$ _____
$3^5 = 243$ _____

What if there's no little number in the log? *You use 10.*

$\log 100 = 2$ *really says* $\log_{10} 100 = 2$

Matrices are just ugly ways of organizing a bunch of numbers. The beauty of matrices on the ACT is that you can almost ALWAYS use your calculator.

- What is the matrix product of $\begin{bmatrix} 2 \\ 4 \\ 3 \end{bmatrix} \cdot \begin{bmatrix} 10 & 1 & 8 \end{bmatrix}$

1. Hit MATRIX on your calculator.
2. Tab over to EDIT and hit ENTER on [A].
3. Select the dimensions of the given matrix

   (Hint: The matrix below should look identical to the problem).
4. Enter your numbers.
5. Repeat as needed with [B], [C], etc.

To USE the matrices you've entered:

1. Hit 2nd QUIT.
2. Hit MATRIX.
3. Select the matrices you want to use under NAMES.
4. Practice on the problem above!

● ●

>>> Trickier Matrices

What is the product of $\begin{bmatrix} 2 \\ 4 \\ 3 \end{bmatrix} \bullet \begin{bmatrix} x & y & z \end{bmatrix}$

A. $\begin{bmatrix} 2x & 4y & 3z \end{bmatrix}$

B. $\begin{bmatrix} 3x & 4y & 2z \end{bmatrix}$

C. $\begin{bmatrix} 2x & 2y & 2z \\ 4x & 4y & 4z \\ 3x & 3y & 3z \end{bmatrix}$

D. $\begin{bmatrix} 2x & 3y & 4z \\ 2x & 3y & 4z \\ 2x & 3y & 4z \end{bmatrix}$

E. $\begin{bmatrix} 0 \end{bmatrix}$

>> STRATEGY

Any time that you see a series of variables, try plugging in. In this case, make a table with three different integer values for x, y, z.

If you haven't taken pre-cal, then the idea of radians is meaningless, but that doesn't mean you can't get the problems right. You just need a couple of important facts and formulas. Then, we'll put the rest in your calculator!

FACTS:

180° = π radians, or halfway around a circle
A full circle is 2π radians.

FORMULAS:
To go from radians to degrees, multiply by

$$\frac{180}{\pi}$$

To go from degrees to radians, multiply by

$$\frac{\pi}{180}$$

Which of the following is equivalent to 1620°?
     A. 3π
     B. 5π
     C. 7π
     D. 9π
     E. 11π

Which of the following is equivalent to $\frac{11\pi}{5}$
     A. 198°
     B. 245°
     C. 396°
     D. 542°
     E. 724°

Now, that's a big, long word that simply means, "measuring 3 sided figures," so why does the sound of it inspire fear? Because you don't know the basics. And, that's why we're here!

Here's a non-word you must know: **SOHCAHTOA**

What does it stand for???

Sine =

Cosine =

Tangent =

So, how is this important to us? Well, Trigonometry deals with right triangles and how their sides and angles relate. We're going to be dealing with those functions above quite a bit, but first, let's label this triangle:

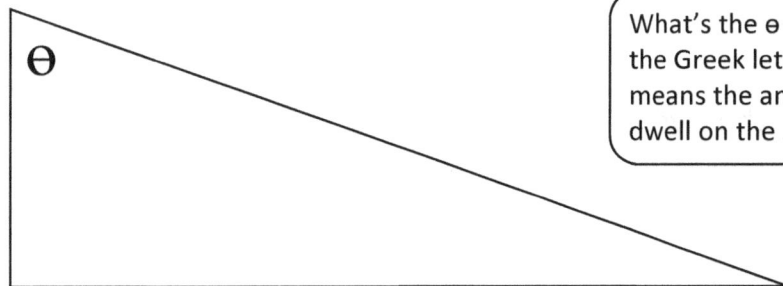

What's the ϴ all about? It's just the Greek letter "theta," and it means the angle measure. Don't dwell on the small stuff!

Sin ϴ =	Cos ϴ =	Tan ϴ =

In the right triangle pictured below, side AC = 10. What is the value of side BC?

A. 6.5
B. 7.2
C. 8.1
D. 10.3
E. 13.8

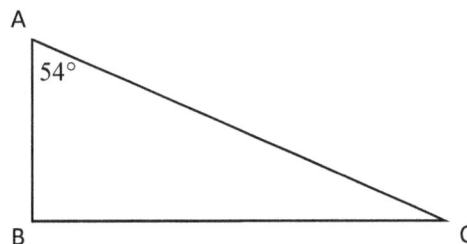

- The ACT loves to put numbers in a series and have you figure out their relationship; sometimes, they'll even want you to add them all up. When it comes to sequences, we'll go over strategies here. When it comes to sums, you should hug your calculator tightly.

>>> Sequences: Arithmetic v. Geometric

Arithmetic sequences have a common **difference**:

Essentially, some number is added or subtracted to get to the next term.

13, 15, __, __, 21

Geometric sequences have a common **ratio**:

Now, you're multiplying or dividing to get to the next term.

64, 32, __, __, 4

What are the two missing terms in the arithmetic sequence below?

64, __, __, 100?

    A. 72, 86
    B. 74, 86
    C. 72, 88
    D. 74, 88
    E. 76, 88

> Remember, you have to have the SAME difference between the terms!

● ●

>>> Sequences: Hello, Calculator!

Most sequence problems on the ACT follow this formula:

$$S_n = n\left(\frac{a_1 + a_n}{2}\right)$$

However, we're not going to dwell on that mess because you can do the whole thing in your calculator!

>> Now... let's do a problem.

Alexander wants to compete in the annual Nathan's hot dog eating competition on the Fourth of July in NYC, so 52 days ago, he began practicing. On the first day, he ate 4 hot dogs, and each day, he increased his consumption by 2 hot dogs. On the 52nd day, he ate 106 hot dogs. How many hot dogs did he eat throughout those 52 days?

    A. 400
    B. 644
    C. 1232
    D. 1816
    E. 2860

● ●

The basic circle equation is:

$$r^2 = (x - h)^2 + (y - k)^2$$

The center of the circle is *(h,k)*.
The equation always equals the radius **squared**.

The circle with center (4, 5) has a radius of 7. What is the equation of this circle?

A. $7 = (x + 5)^2 + (y + 4)^2$

B. $7 = (x - 5)^2 + (y - 4)^2$

C. $7 = (x - 4)^2 + (y - 5)^2$

D. $49 = (x + 4)^2 + (y + 5)^2$

E. $49 = (x - 4)^2 + (y - 5)^2$

ACT READING

READING

BREAKDOWN...

40 multiple-choice questions based on 4 passages in only 35 minutes.

Each passage has 10 questions

The Reading section of the ACT is time sensitive!

If you were to attempt to complete all 4 passages, that's only about 8 minutes per passage. Before you panic, we will set up an attack strategy to help you get through this section as quickly and as accurately as possible.

● ●

The ACT presents the same four types of passages in the same order for every test. The order for the passages is as follows:

Prose Fiction >> Social Sciences >> Humanities >> Natural Sciences

● ●

For the ACT Reading, there are 5 Table Turning Techniques that can help you to master this section .

1.

2.

3.

4.

5.

" The ACT does not measure whether or not you are a "good" or "fast" reader. The goal of this course is to learn the techniques that work well for this test and this test ONLY. Don't let the testmakers get you down! We know that they are testing you on how well you take this one test, that's it. "

1   KNOW YOUR STRENGTHS

- Remember, the Reading section's passages are always in the following order: Prose Fiction, Social Sciences, Humanities, and Natural Sciences.
- You don't have to do the passages in this order. Do the passages that you find easier to do first and save the toughest one for last.

2   READ TO REFER BACK, NOT TO REMEMBER

- You don't have time to fully become engaged in the passage and remember all the details. You should spend no more than 4 or 5 minutes skimming the passage.

- Once you finish, go to your questions and refer to the section of the passage that information is in.

3   MARK UP YOUR PASSAGE

- The questions are not in order nor are there lots of line references.
- In order to be able to refer back, circle, underline, or notate your passages. This makes it easier for you to locate the correct answers.

what you should do

4 PREDICT, THEN ELIMINATE

- It is easier to prove answer choices wrong than it is to prove correct.
- Get into the habit of reading the question, referring back to the passage, and then eliminating the answer choices you know are wrong.

5 WATCH FOR TRAPS

- Test makers word answer choices in tricky ways. They will put key words in each answer choice, knowing that these words will "jog your memory."
- Don't fall for the traps. You must first know what the answer should be in order to eliminate good ones.

>> STRATEGY

You must answer these questions strategically. Many students eliminate answer choices because they don't like the choices or they don't understand how the answer choice could work. Neither one is a good reason to eliminate an answer. **You must be able to prove it wrong.**

RIGHT AND WRONG

- Right answer choices may not "look right." Correct answer choices are basically paraphrases of the passage. By first putting the answer in your own words, it will be much easier for you to eliminate the wrong ones.

>>> Types of Wrong Answer Choices

>> **Extreme language:** Language that is too nice or too mean tends to be wrong. Also be on the lookout for answer choices that are too definitive, such as absolutely, impossible, all, and none.

>> **Pointless:** These answer choices have nothing to do with the passage, yet they can be rationalized because they make sense.

>> **Wrong Scope:** These answers are either too vague or too specific.

>> **Identical Wording:** These tend to be the trickiest ones because these contain key words you are more likely to remember from the passage, yet these answer choices do not mean the same thing as what was mentioned in the passage.

● ●

KNOW WHAT TO LOOK FOR

- Standardized tests are predictable. No matter what type of information the passages contain, the test will always ask you the same types of questions.

>>> Passage Questions:

While not exactly like the questions you will encounter on the test, the following are the general types of questions:

>> Identify specific **facts** and **details**

>> Identify the **meaning of a word** used in a certain context

>> Identify **cause-and effect** relationships

>> Make **comparisons**

>> Identify the character's personality **characteristics** and **goals** and **struggles**

>> Identify the **main idea**

>> Identify the **pros and cons** of an issue

>> Identify the writer's **reason for writing** the passage

SAT
ACT

TURN THE TABLES ON THE TEST-MAKERS

ACT SCIENCE

SCICENCE

BREAKDOWN...

40 multiple-choice questions based on 7 passages in 35 minutes.

Like the Reading, the Science is also time sensitive.

The stark reality is, that's sometimes not enough time to finish all of the passages, but THAT'S OKAY!!

You just have to make the most of the time, and do as many as possible. Your job is to read through the nonsense and beat them at their own game!

Silly Science, we see through your tricks!!

The Science may be the most dreaded section of this test because it seems different, unfamiliar, and unpredictable. In truth, it's just an extension of the reading section – this version just includes numbers and experiments.

CHARTS AND GRAPHS

- Can you read charts and graphs? Of course, you can. You've been doing it since first grade.

\>> Check out this exercise to understand how temperature affects Marge Simpson's hair:

Experiment 1:

A group of students made Marge Simpson stand outside in a variety of temperatures. Each day, they measured the height of her hair (See Table 1).

Table 1

Study	Temperature (degrees Fahrenheit)	Height of the fro (inches)
1	72	29
2	78	34
3	61	24
4	95	50

Based on the information provided in Table 1, what relationship may be deduced between Marge's hair height and the temperature?

A. As temperature increases, the height decreases.
B. As temperature increases, the height increases.
C. As temperature decreases, the height increases.
D. As temperature, the height increases and then decreases.

Suppose the students were to measure Marge's hair in 84 degree weather. Which would be an appropriate estimate of the height on that day in inches?

F. 22
G. 26
H. 31
J. 42

Because of the students' Marge Simpson hair study, a group of teachers became interested in how the diameter of Marge's hair might change if substances were added to it.

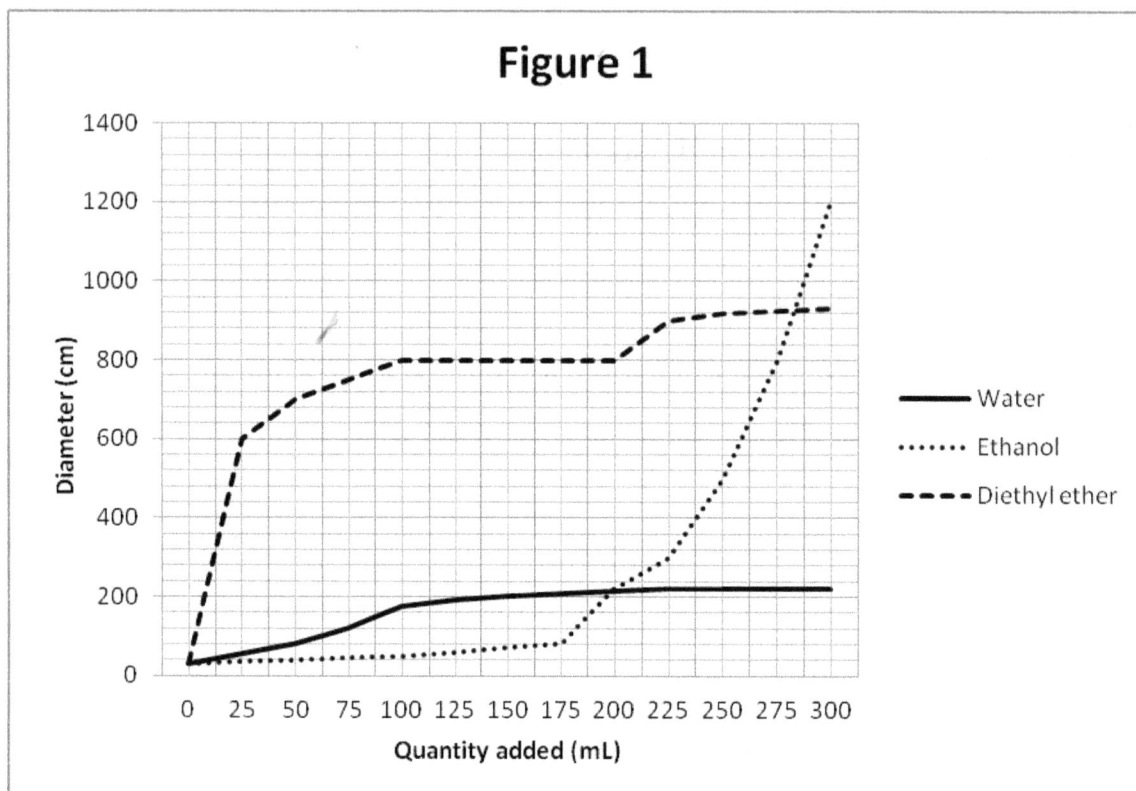

Figure 1

1. What is the approximate diameter of Marge's hair when 65 mL of water have been added?
   A. 50
   B. 100
   C. 150
   D. 200

2. Which of the following is true about the effect of ethanol on the diameter of Marge's hair?
   F. The diameter stays relatively constant until 75 mL have been added and then escalates rapidly.
   G. The diameter stays relatively constant until 130 mL have been added and then escalates rapidly.
   H. The diameter stays relatively constant until 175 mL have been added and then escalates rapidly.
   J. The diameter stays relatively constant until 250 mL have been added and then escalates rapidly.

- Okay, so the Science section doesn't really talk about Marge's hair. It talks about *vaporization constants* and *spent fuel* and *thermodynamic equilibrium* because those are scientific terms.

- But 95% of the time, the scientific terms themselves <u>don't matter at all</u>! The numbers, processes, and opinions do!

• •

You can expect to find three types of passages on the Science section.

1

2

3

STUDY PASSAGES

- Some passages present a few different studies, along with a few charts or graphs.
- There are 3 of these passages, each with 5 questions.
- TOTAL = 15 questions

EXPERIMENT PASSAGES

- Other passages package up a few different charts and graphs in the context of a big research project, detailing different experiments and their results.
- There are 3 of these passages, each with 6 questions.
- Total = 18 questions

>>> Basic info on Study and Experiment Passages:

The questions deal with the data. You generally do **NOT** have to read the passages!

You will usually have to do one of three things:

>> **Read the chart or graph to come up with a specific piece of data (Question 1 on the graph about the diameter of Marge's hair).**

>> **Make inferences (Question 2 on the chart about the height of Marge's hair).**

>> **Interpret relationships among the data (Question 1 on the chart about the height of Marge's hair).**

- Preview the passage BRIEFLY.
- Underline any *italicized* terms.
- Go to the questions.
- Tackle the questions that deal with one passage at a time first.
- Then, move onto the more detailed questions.
- Use the data to answer the questions.

3   ARGUMENT PASSAGES

- There's just **one** of these on each test.
- It has **seven** questions.
- It's basically a short reading comp passage.

>>> How is the argument set up?

>> Well, it's like this. One scientist thinks one thing; a second scientist thinks the opposite.

>> If the ACT people want to get really fancy, they might toss in a quick third guy at the end, just to give another perspective. That's about as creative as these guys get.

Introduction to the topic

Scientist 1 says, "I think this, and here's why!"

Scientist 2 says, "Don't listen to that joker. I know the truth, and here's why!"

And, if it's fancy-pants time, Scientist 3 will ring in, "But have you thought about this?!"

>> STRATEGY

- Figure out _____ by reading the _____.
- Underline _____ opinion and mark his _____.
- Underline _____ opinion and mark his _____.
- In those rare cases, underline what Scientist 3 thinks he's contributing by speaking up!

>>> What will the questions cover?

>> Details about each scientist's beliefs.

>> Points where the scientists agree.

>> Points where the scientists disagree.

> Now, let's practice with a full passage >

American scientists have recently identified a Smurf colony in the heart of the Maine countryside. Until now, scientists have observed the little blue creatures with a high-powered telescope. Scientists have been most intrigued by the Smurfs' dwellings, which are indeed located within the stems and caps of red-and-white button mushrooms, known as *Amanita smurfaria*. Alternating bands of gray and white *tubular strata* appear on the outer layer of the stems. Two scientists express their views about whether the physical features observed are indicative of an advanced hydrostatic pressure system within the hyphae of the mushrooms.

Scientist 1

Just beneath the skin of the *Amanita smurfaria* lies a body of thick veins and arteries, which buffer the mushroom hyphae against the stresses and pressures of internal home construction and daily living within the mushroom body. These circulatory vessels resemble those in the human body because of their alternating layers of muscle, both circular and longitudinal. The *tubular strata* result from the interactions of these muscular layers when the fungus copes with stress, drawing extra water to maintain enough pressure to retain its shape.

An advanced biological hydrostatic system would cause the portions of the stem bearing an extra load to undergo a bulging effect, primarily around the second-story window level. We have confirmed that such bulges exist.

Scientist 2

Amanita smurfaria's circulatory hydrostatic capabilities are not exceptional. Any advanced pressure system would prevent the Smurf builders from creating sufficient living spaces because the forces would be exerted in both inward and outward directions, leaving the inhabitants vulnerable to an implosion of their homes. The *tubular strata* actually are indicative of a unique chemical composition, which allows the *Amanita smurfaria* to transform its hyphae into pier-like structures, providing the support necessary to allow habitation. Those structures would necessarily result in surface bulging because of their compositional differences.

1. Which of the following best describes how the 2 scientists explain the bulges on the mushrooms' surfaces?

	Scientist 2	Scientist 1
A.	Inward pressure	Outward pressure
B.	Chemical changes	Physical changes
C.	Water buildup	Physical changes
D.	Physical changes	Chemical changes

2. According to the information provided, both of the scientists would agree on which statement?

F. The intense pressure demanded by the Smurfs' dwellings requires the allocation of cell resources to enhancing vessel musculature.

G. The circulatory vessels of *Amanita smurfaria* have alternating layers of longitudinal and circular muscle.

H. The bulging structures apparent on the surface of *Amanita smurfaria* correlate with the tensions caused from Smurf habitat development.

J. The pier-like transformations of the hyphae provide the structural composition to sustain life within the mushroom bodies.

3. Based on Scientist 1's views, which of the following must occur in order to produce the *tubular strata*?

A. Intense pressure
B. Interactions of muscular layers
C. Window construction
D. Hydrostatic development

4. Assume that Scientist 1's comparison of the mushroom's musculature and human musculature, is accurate. Based on this assumption, then humans under intense strain would be *least* likely to display which of the following?

F. Banded flesh
G. Above-average pressure
H. Physical breakage
J. Visible bulges at the site of stress

5. Which of the following best summarizes the source of the scientists' disagreement?

A. The cause of the apparent *tubular strata*
B. The extreme pressure experienced by *Amanita smurfaria*
C. The ability of the mushroom to adapt
D. The structural composition of the Smurfs' homes

6. Which of the following statements about *Amanita smurfaria* would be consistent with both scientists' views?

F. The mushroom's overall physiology differs from that of other known mushrooms.
G. The chemistry of *Amanita smurfaria* is unique.
H. Smurf dwellings can direct hydrostatic pressure in only one direction.
J. The Smurf living spaces must be extremely small.

7. In response to Scientist 1, Scientist 2 would reply that he had made which of the following errors?

A. Misunderstood the nature of water pressure
B. Overlooked a very likely outcome of such intense pressure
C. Improperly assigned human characteristics to a nonhuman entity.
D. Exaggerated the size of the mushrooms' surface bulges.

www.ingramcontent.com/pod-product-compliance
Lightning Source LLC
Chambersburg PA
CBHW081212020426
42331CB00012B/2998